THE ABUNDANCE WAY

Don't Go Belly Up While Getting Rich

By

Jackie w. chapman

Copyright@2023

DISCLAIMER

Copyright © by Francis bailey 2023. All rights reserved. Before this document is duplicated or reproduced in any manner, the publisher's consent must be gained. Therefore, the contents within can neither be stored electronically, transferred, nor kept in a database. Neither in Part nor full can the document be copied, scanned, faxed, or retained without approval from the publisher or creator

About the author

Jackie w.chapman is a "Writer, historian, and activist. Jackie is the author of the book knowing yourself Which is the first book she is writing and it is about human interaction with oneself. She loveseverything about power, uprisings, art, environment, place, pleasure, politics, hope, and cooking. She is hoping to further her career in the nearest future.

Table of content

CHAPTER1
- Mentality
- What is a Mentality?

Chapter2
- Chance and Award Remain forever inseparable

Chapter3
- Discipline is the way to progress

Chapter4
- Why it is critical to stop the examination game

Chapter5
- How The Law Of Correspondence Applies To Business Achievement

Chapter6
- You Don't Need Additional Time, You Simply Have to Spend It Doing What Is important

CHAPTER7
- KNOW YOURSELF

chapter8
- Wealth:true importance of riches
- What Is Abundance?

CHAPTER 9
- There is continuously a new thing to learn

CHAPTER 10
- Set your cash to work

CHAPTER 11
- Your wellbeing is your most noteworthy abundance and resource

INTRODUCTION

The Way to Genuine Riches

I have been around many individuals with all the cash and status one could dream of, the hotshot" who sanction a confidential plane to their favored abroad store they have saved so they could search for their new jewel studded Rolex in harmony. However these equivalent people carry on with an everyday presence that reflects everything except genuine riches. In the background, their lives are an utter trainwreck: their relationships are a catastrophe, their wellbeing is wrecked, and they have no confidence or reason directing their speculation of time, energy, and cash, nothing to legitimize the "hustle" that characterizes their personality. They have sought after monetary overflow to the detriment of everything except theirego, and the outcome? They are broken, and they are broken. Time and again, pseudo-values like hustle, efficiency, and benefit are put on the most elevated platform in the business world. In any case, for the individual whose values run further, these are, best case scenario, means to more noteworthy finishes, devices to support the genuine wellsprings of importance. Those with a more noteworthy reason hustle when that prompts them since they see a need that they have the assets and capacity to meet. They seek after benefits that will extend their ability to serve. Failing to focus on the more profound why" when you're drenched in the way of life of business, business venture, or the one where I started out, land investing is very much simple." In the event that you're not purposefully focusing on your qualities, making your business your god is simple. However my expert life has advanced emphatically throughout the past ten years, my qualities and my confidence have stayed the constants, the establishments on which all else is assembled. I flipped my most memorable home in 2015. Presently, after seven years, I flip many houses and purchase hundred or more unit high rises. I run seven organizations with the assistance of the group of whizzes that I utilize. I produce web-based entertainment content consistently for north of 1,000,000 adherents. Notwithstanding all of this, I invest more energy with my family than any time in recent memory, more than at the point when I was battling to keep my head above water. I'm more associated with my congregation than ever. I'm sound. I'm cheerful. What I have is valid riches, the sort that doesn't vacillate helpless before my ledger equilibrium or stock portfolio. This book, and the course that preceded it, is, to some extent, the result of various inquiries and criticism I got from my supporters who considered how I could deal with these ventures while likewise keeping a solid everyday life and a solid confidence. They needed to know how I got it done, and I needed to offer individuals another way, an existence of abundance that stretches out past the thoughtless quest for cash. I needed to show individuals that planning, for instance, shouldn't matter just to cash. All things considered, genuine thriving is the result of planning your chance to put resources into every part of the way of life you wish to lead and the individual you need to turn into. This was my motivation for the Abundance abbreviation, each letter addressing one part of the really bountiful life: love, schooling, luxuriousness, way of life, group, and wellbeing. To some extent three of this book, we'll talk about each essential component of genuine abundance top to bottom. For the present, what's critical to understand thus frequently neglected is that there is something else to life besides cash. Obviously, this abbreviation incorporates A for monetary wealth, yet I've seen extremely many individuals go through years pursuing cash just to find that it is an unfilled objective since they ignored different regions that add to a significant life. In this book, I will detail bit by bit and rule by-guideline my way to deal with life, business, and cash. I will frame my everyday practice and the job of the Abundance abbreviation at its establishment, alongside every one of the manners in which I financial plan and contribute my opportunity to make a satisfying life. I made the Affluent Way since I profoundly wanted to share the delight and development it has brought to my life. The Rich Way is a local area; it is a way of thinking, a tool stash, and a diagram. It is the summit of the ups and downs of my excursion that eventually prompted the achievement I have tracked down today, and I really accept that the standards you will track down here hold the possibility to completely change you and impact the world.

CHAPTER 1

Mentality

What is a Mentality?

A mentality is a focal point through which you view the world. Like a couple of shades, it can marginally modify what you see and your opinion on it. Mentalities are included convictions, discernments, and perspectives that illuminate your contemplations and choices. Various attitudes are a significant piece of your toolbox for progress. Like glasses, they can darken your way or carry lucidity to the street ahead. Developing a sound abundance outlook will assist you with adhering to your monetary objectives and track down ways of expanding your procuring potential.

What is an abundance mentality?

In the event that you dig further into the narratives of well off individuals, you'll see a theme: Seldom can a well off individual reduce their prosperity to a solitary supernatural second. All things being equal, they'll refer to their mentality as the main motivation for their flourishing. An abundance outlook is a bunch of convictions, propensities, and ways of behaving that isolates the well off from the rest. An abundance outlook will direct you to capitalize on the cash you have.

In any case, it doesn't come simple. An abundance outlook implies spending less, making wise speculations, and searching for ways of working on monetary remaining with insignificant gamble.
Fortunately with just enough commitment, anybody can foster this attitude.

What is an Unfortunate Mentality?

The direct opposite of an abundance mentality is an unfortunate outlook. Most who have this "unfortunate mentality" don't understand they have poor unfortunate attitude is any of the accompanying: feeling that bringing in cash is off-base, that it very well may be managed without exertion, that you won't ever move out of the pit of obligation, or that you simply don't have the exceptional sauce it takes to increment cash blossoms mentality subverts your cash objectives and will effectively drive abundance away from you except if you work to balance it.

For what reason does an abundance mentality matter?

60% of Americans live check to check — and it possibly deteriorates when we consider the rising degrees of Visa obligation. Starting around 2018, 175 million Americans effectively use Visas. A larger part of these Visa holders participate in imprudent spending conduct, squandering cash they don't have on things they needn't bother with. These ways of behaving make horrible twisters of obligation from which it is challenging to escape. It appears to be that the capacity to accomplish riches — the fundamentals of the abundance mentality — is an under-appreciated skill.

4Step in getting an abundance outlook

1. Put forth Objectives, Show restraint, Endure

Not very many well off individuals became rich short-term. Creating financial wellbeing is a sluggish interaction.
Facebook didn't transform Imprint Zuckerberg into a very rich person. Mark Zuckerberg made Facebook with his diligent, effort and dedication then, at that point, and afterward received the rewards of his work. Try not to stick your expectations of accomplishing abundance on dangerous "make easy money" adventures. The typical affluent individual invests multiple times more energy arranging their funds than the typical working class person.
Put forth an objective for the amount you will save every month. All the more critically — ensure that the arrangement you make for yourself is sensible and stick to it. The motivation behind a spending plan is to permit you to inspect your costs and search for regions where you can reduce or take out expenses. This cycle could expect you to go with a few hard choices, such as changing to less expensive forms of items or keeping away from extravagances out and out. In the event that you're horrible at saving and you plan to save 10% of your next check, you have a higher possibility of falling flat angivinggup living your mission to become well off. For what reason doesn't begin at 1%? Begin little, sustain the propensity, and scale up after some time.

2. Put resources into what's in store

today generally feel that cash would make itself... Or will it? Build revenue is a course of development that permits your put away cash to develop dramatically after some time. Accumulate revenue happens when you procure interest on interest. Every year your cash is contributed, you'll procure a level of revenue on the aggregate sum of cash in the record, which incorporates the sum you made the year before. The more you permit your record to develop, the more cash you will make consequently. In 1994, Bill Doors was valued at 9.3 billion bucks. Quick forward to 2014 and the man was valued at 81.6 billion bucks. This nine-crease expansion in abundance wasn't energized byMicrosoft deals alone. It was fueled by Bill GatesGates'sstments director Michael Larson. Putting away cash is a central technique among well off individuals — and you don't need to do it single-handedly. Figure out how to contribute or search for help. There are a lot of achieved and reliable counselors out there.

The reality? Letting every one of your reserve funds sit inactive in a ledger is a serious mix-up. Confections used to be 5 pennies a pop. Today, you'd be unable to purchase a Snickers for under a dollar. The supported expansion in costs over the long haul for labor and products is called expansion. It diminishes the buying influence of cash over the long haul.

On the off chance that your speculation system is to leave your cash in a bank account for quite a long time, your savings will be worth very much less when you're at last prepared to utilize it.

All things considered, gauge your venture choices. Normal techniques for effective money management incorporate 401ks and Roth IRAs.

A 401k is a retirement plan that you can put resources into yourself or through your boss. It is possible that you put cash in it every month yourself, or a little piece of your check is taken out each payroll interval and put resources into the financial exchange. Businesses can match your commitments, and your cash will keep on developing until you choose to get to it in your brilliant years. Since commitments are made on a pre-charge premise — the cash you put in can decrease your available pay for that year — you will pay personal duty on it when you haul the cash out.

One more choice is a Roth IRA, subsidized by after-charge dollars. Thus, when you haul this cash out, you need to make good on no duty, however you can't diminish your available pay in the present.

An abundance mentality can assist you with searching out the best speculations for your necessities. All things considered, who would rather not bring in cash while they rest?

3. Hustle constantly

Since you have an establishment for developing your cash, now is the right time to put resources into the main thing Yourself.

To cultivate an abundance outlook, you'll have to limit time-squandering exercises like sitting in front of the TV or looking at online entertainment. Internationally, we spend more than two hours via virtual entertainment destinations consistently. Rather than burning through that time looking over, deal with your body. On the off chance that you're not previously zeroing in on your psychological and actual wellbeing, learn and rehearse "better wellbeing propensities", like practicing good eating habits, resting right, and practicing the correct way. Here is another thought: practice your discussion abilities. Whether it's arranging your bills, your, salary,y or, a client contract, rich individuals generally beat the competition and are acaneze more dollars for themselves.

Make money as an afterthought by making a part time job. By driving for a ride-sharing help, showing courses on the web, or in any event, directing weddings, 44 million Americans procure a normal of $25 each hour with a side gig.

Find a specialty you're energetic about and it won't actually feel like work.

Master new abilities in regions you're keen on as well. No one can tell when an expertise you mastered today will turn into an open door later down the line.

4. Keep an uplifting outlook

Perhaps you've known about the "pattern of good following good." The pattern of energy attracting similar energy expresses that like draws in like. As such, our considerations and activities draw in comparative contemplations and activities. Assuming you figure positive considerations, positive things will occur. On the off chance that you contemplate making abundance, you will bring more abundance into your life. You should encourage positive considerations of riches and overflow. Assuming you harp on the negative, you'll get deterred and abandon your fantasies. Begin by deleting negative considerations from your brain. Supplant them with considerations like:
"I will be rich."
"I'm adequate."
"I can succeed."
The way to abundance is difficult, however it will not be any more straightforward assuming you begin making potholes for yourself. You should be totally sold on the possibility of your prosperity.

What amount of time Does it Require for To Foster An Abundance Outlook?

The most amazing aspect of fostering an abundance mentality is that you can begin right away — by training, planning, and afterward activity. The key is to begin little and tackle scaled down objectives first. Like self multiplying dividends, these little speculations develop after some time and further your advancement toward your abundance goals. Within months, weeks, or even days, your abundance objectives will be on the road to success to progress.

Get It Going

There's no straightforward equation to follow for abundance. Perhaps you'll have a splendid thought and own it. Perhaps you'll begin a business with an incredible prime supporter. Perhaps, as the majority of us, you'll really buckle down — however save shrewd and put your direction into wealth. By the day's end, everybody needs to take the course that is appropriate for them. Be that as it may, the people who come to the end will be the people who scallop and adhere to the abundance attitude.

CHAPTER 2

Chance and Award Remain forever inseparable

"Never permit the anxiety toward striking out your you from forming the game."
-Darling RUTH

Research demonstrates that your body and mind eventually follow the walking requests of your will. A concentrate out of Finland looked at the design and enactment examples of the minds of low and high-daring people.' The specialists calculated that the generally safe takers faltered in settling on decisions so they could consider the savviest game-plan. In view of that supposition, they expected to track down this gathering to have more perplexing brain organizations; at the end of the day, they felt that they would be more brilliant. They wound up viewing it as the inverse. Collectively, the daring people showed fundamentally more white matter than the individuals who would in general leave nothing to chance. Basically, white matter is the expressway arrangement of the mind, the streets that permit data to travel openly and deftly from one area to another. More white matter, then, at that point, implies more perplexing thought. Also, that implies more workarounds, similar to an intricate thruway framework where you can choose elective courses to arrive at your ideal objective. The daring people had brain networks like a guide of my old neighborhood of Las Vegas: the gamble avoiders .indeed, their minds seemed to be the sluggish desert towns a short drive from the neon lights of the city. However, how could this be? Couldn't we expect that the reasonable ones who think about each possible result prior to acting could be the shrewd ones? Not in the event that their circumspection brings about loss of motion. By definition, we don't have the foggiest idea what we will find when we adventure into an obscure area, and dangers generally go with difficulties. In any case, similar to the body that never works since it never leaves the sofa, the mind that never experiences the difficulties that follow takes a chance with stays immature. The cerebrums of daring individuals are more evolved on the grounds that they seek changes. They don't lounge around thinking about every one of the results and potential outcomes. They proceed to figure out what they are really going after. Experience a snag? A gridlock? The daring individuals track down one more strategy for getting around, and on the off chance that there isn't one, they pass through the grass until another way is worn. They believe that they can adjust, and as it should be. The will provides the walking orders, and the brain and body follow. Abundance Manufacturers. Those rich take action with reasons to stay trapped in uncertainty that never prompts activity, utilization that never means creation, and arranging that never sums to execution. The point that appears to be so self-evident yet is missed by so many is that you don't go anywhere by stopping in the present time and place, always pondering what you'll do when there and afterward arrive. The benefit of "here" for the people who stay away from chances is that it appears to be protected. What you know is what you can see, smell, taste, contact, and that's just the beginning or less foresee in view of your propensities, the same ways you answer exactly the same things you see a large number of days. However, actually on the grounds that you decide to wait doesn't mean all the other things will; "here" will constantly prompt some obscure whether or not you decide to partake. Yet, where you end up doesn't necessarily take a risk completely. You are not defenseless in that frame of mind to impact the outCoutcometimately, you concludes whether the spot that you happens ns to you, similar to weeds springing up as you sit inactively in hesitation and inaction or through the flame of natural products spring form your choices and activities. Valid, nothing is ensured, however you work on the probability of getting what you need from the future assuming you steer steps that way. Unavoidably, you pick your gamble.

Taking a chance with Openness

The gamble avoider's reluctance to go up against their apprehension about the obscure leaves them accidentally disabled. Despite the fact that they could feel discontent with their ongoing conditions, exhausted, desolate, and tainted by life in a one-stoplight town, they reason that essentially it is protected here. Their discontent is offset by the apprehension that they will get gobbled up assuming they adventure beyond what they know, so they sit idle. Furthermore, accomplishing nothing could attempt to guarantee wellbeing temporarily. Without a doubt, it would be terrifying to have a go at a genuinely new thing. However, prepare to have your mind blown. Dread feeds on evasion. However, the inverse is likewise evident. The fix the because of a paranoid fear of facing challenges is equivalent to for some other trepidation: openness. At the point when an individual searches out the help of a specialist to defeat a fear bugs, suppose then they will steadily expose some hehee sentationtion of insects until they understand anything horrendous result they envisioned would happen in the event that they experience a bug never really occurs. Thus, for instance, a specialist could begin by empowering the arachnophobe to just envision and examine what it might be want to experience an insect, an activity that at first could excite a fair setup of dread yet inevitably turns out to be very unarousing, in any event, exhausting. Then, the specialist could have him watch a video of an insect. From that point forward, he will notice the live spider from another annotated the same room. At last, the individual who at first accepted he was unequipped for bearing to such an extent as the possibility of bugs might find that he can permit one to creep on his arm without result or dread. As such, what at first appeared to be unimaginably dangerous ended up being very unremarkable. At last, each step of openness requires a demonstration of trust that you can deal with anything that impediments and difficulties might emerge as you step into the unexplored world. What's more, confidence, whether in God or yourself, fills in as a method and an end. Confidence powers the will to act and actinactingher energizes theuelsthe confidence that motivates the activities to come: bolder ones with more serious dangers and more noteworthy prizes. Incidentally, confidence goes before and continues the will to act. Actitemstems At the underpinning of all fears la its dangers: chance of disappointment, hazard of embarrassment, chance of letting completely go, right down to the gamble of death. When combined with aversion, that dread misrepresents each gamble and envisioned outcome until no award past the security of the state of affairs appears to be sensible. However, truly risk additionally goes with each extraordinary victory not win over dread but rather win regardless of dread. Belis are a few different ways that you can embrace gambles even with dread and find the prizes that lie past business as usual:

1. Track down a second job. Loveseat flipping, hosechose clippingisharingoceryocery looking for others-the choices are unending. Which begins as additional pay might very much turn out to be sufficient to earn enough to pay the bills. This is the everyday issue where you can attempt new things and trial. Begin little and scale.

2. Embrace openness. Like arachnophobes The Will to Take a chance with I showed up back home with the sofa close behind and, no doubt stirring up a lot of disappointment for my better half, packed it into the generally restricted space of our little condo. The time had come to test my hypothesis. I gave the love seat a little spot-cleaning, snapped a couple photographs, and posted it right back on Craigslist for 300 bucks more than whatever I paid for it. A couple of days after the fact, the lounge chair sold at the asking value, no inquiries posed. That was my moment of realization. The gamble of venturing out on trust to take a stab at something totally new had paid off, and that was all the confirmation I expected to go greater and bolder. In practically no time, I had taken what little we had set aside and purchased an old beat-up GMC Sierra (that I later found had a changed odometer that showed far less miles than she lly voyaged) for fifteen hundred bucks, leased a 10x30 stockpiling unit to hold my stock, and was making excellent progress so far on my initial introduction to business. Right out of the entryway, lounge chair flipping was a triumph. I purchased and exchanged all that I could find that was underestimated and brought on the month and realize sizes a Search..pretty rapidly that my profit were restricted exclusively by my capacity to store all that I purchased. So I went greater. I extended to multiple capacity units to stay aware of interest. I sorted out what kind of love seat presented to it the most benefits (it's sectionals, coincidentally). Feeling like a major clock, I even moved up to the 2004 Toyota Tundra that I would supplant and provide for my father a couple of years after the fact. 1,000 bucks became 2,000, 2,000 became four until ultimately, I created eight thousanddolthousaninnt gain each and every month. What started as a trial had transformed into an undeniable living. Regardless of getting more cash than I at any point had and doing t own terms, achievement included some major disadvantages. I began to get worn out. At the point when I was simply beginning any expectations of making the significant associations had been run by my delivery from the A's, and I had arrived at the end of unfulfilling long and fruitless stretch as a realtor. With the stakes high and my certainty low, purchasing a solitary love seat to exchange introduced a gamble, to our small investment funds as well as to my swollen self image. So making money on it seemed like a daily existence radeliveringring an invigorating delivery. I could relax. This offered a transitory help toward the back of dissatisfaction, a restored ability to know east from west, and fast, solid benefits; it advertised "achievement." After a year, I had a full-scale business with a conveyance truck, numerous capacity canisters, and enough couchoneo fill eonaallwthew thethellowlallspite that purchasing a couch became ... exhausting, such as watching a bug creep around in the following room. Other than that, lounge chair flipping was a drudgery, one that at first outgrew desperation and need and one expected as a second job, not a final plan. I held no fancies of flipping lounge chairs as a vocation. Certainly, I had started to find what felt like monetary flourishing given the shortage I had become used to, yet between nally, I realized something was astray. Set forth plainly, I was not glad for what I was doing, and I knew in my heart that I was intended for something else. It was the ideal opportunity for a shift in course, yet I was no more clear about where to go than I had been a year prior to when I had left on this insane love seat flipping venture. This inward anxiety finished when Mindy and I visited New Orleans for our most memorable commemoration. A year removed from my matter-of-fact discharge from the A's, I got a very much past due breather from the perpetual hustle of flipping sofas. As I pondered my place throughout everyday life, I quieted my tension and went to the Ruler to show me my best course of action. Bowing on the dim rug of our lodging, hands collapsed on the bed, I inquired, "Jesus, how would you believe I should manage my life?" Much to my dismay that I would some time or another think back on that request as the defining moment of my life.

CHAPTER 3

Discipline is the way to progress

Despite what you are attempting to accomplish (independence from the rat race, improved hea, lth or even business achievement, ess), you should have the discipline to keep focused to arrive at your objectives effectively. Having discipline holds you back from being diverted or making indiscreet decisiothatich will rapidly wreck us from achieving our objective.

The greatest hindrance to defeat while attempting to rehearse discipline is the longing for moment delight. The "I must have it now" disorder. Sadly, in the present culture, we are conditioned into accepting that besides the fact that I should have anything I need At this moment, however, I additionally Merit it. This famous attitude has gotten such countless people and families into serious obligations and some of the time that obligation has finished in chapter 11 and tragically even separation.

So how would we learn discipline? How would we get ourselves out of the moment satisfaction brains to areas of strength for accomplish sound monetary wellness? I honestly think following the vital standards underneath will set you up for better progress and assist you with utilizing your discipline muscles.

Three Moves toward making more grounded discipline

Stage 1 - Have a monetary arrangement (and a spending plan)

You can't accomplish any objective without knowing where you are going. Having a decent, useful spending plan will assist you with getting to where you are attempting to wind up. It doesn't make any difference in the event that you are attempting to escape obligation or create financial stability to accomplish both of these monetary objectives, having a plan is basic. Having a financial plan set up will help you in all of your spending choices. With a financial plan, you know the amount you can or can't spend in some random classification. On the off chance that you have no cash left in your feasting out classification, well then you realize you will eat at home. If in any case, you have cash left in that classification and a lot of your companions airheaded out to supper or party time then you can express yes with the information that eating out won't wreck your objectives.
Having an arrangement set up will assist with holding you back from pursuing poor rash choices that will either dial back your growing long term financial stability or impede your capacity to escape obligation

.Stage 2 - Quit attempting to stay aware of the Joneses

For such countless individuals this is the hardest step. It is so natural to become involved with what others are purchasing and doing, and web-based entertainment makes it that a lot harder. While we are diving in and endeavoring to take care of obligation, adhering to our spending plan, we see pictures on Instagram and Facebook of companions purchasing newsportscar RKmarkers,or taking an intricate get-away. Seeing others apparently appreciate lavish ways of life everyday can without much of a stretch compromise one's discipline to keep focused to accomplish their monetary objectives.

Yet, many individuals don't comprehend that the vast majority who purchase new costly vehicles or take very good quality excursions are not rich. They are commonly the ones with the most measure of obligation. Try not to trust me? Here is an incredible blog entry with additional subtleties.
For you to accomplish YOUR objectives you really want to relinquish the present prevalent misconception of who is rich and who isn't, and you want to relinquish attempting to stay aware of your neighbors. Keep in mind, in the event that you are taking care of obligation, you are presumably in an impermanent circumstance. You foster your discipline by tolerating a few momentary penances realizing that not too far off you'll have a drawn out result.

Stage 3 Get a responsibility

Responsibility just means noting or representing your activities and results. What's more, the most ideal way to be considered responsible for your spending and saving is for somebody who loves you enough to come clean with you - somebody who will consider you responsible to your ultimate objectives. This individual can be your mate (for this situation you are responsibility accomplices - you can consider each other responsible), a dear companion, or even a parent.

It can likewise be a monetary mentor such as myself. Notwithstanding what its identity is, they need to adore you enough to let you know what you Want to hear versus what you might Need to hear. It is somebody you can contact Prior to making a huge buy or when you get sidetracked. Meeting on a normal predictable premise with your responsibility accomplice will assist you with remaining consistent with your objectives and assist you with remaining restrained.

How about we wrap it up

Returning to my objective of better living - I'm accomplishing my objectives and remaining restrained on the grounds that I have an arrangement. I track my food and my activity - no mystery. I don't stress over the extraordinary food pictures every one of my companions love to post all over online entertainment since I'm stressed over MY wellbeing and I'm the one that needs to live in this body so I'm the one that requirements to remain restrained to accomplish ideal wellbeing for ME - not my neighbors or any other person.

To the extent that a responsibility accomplice? My significant other. He doesn't take food no longer any of my concern when I go after something not on my eating plan and he doesn't censure me when I skirt the rec center - what he does is empower me and help me to remember my triumphs as a whole. Have I screwed up? Goodness no doubt. In any case, I didn't surrender. I have fostered a more elevated level of discipline through training. Reliably rehearsing discipline is vital to accomplishing generally more prominent monetary wellness

CHAPTER 4

Why it is critical to stop the examination game

The grass isn't greener on the opposite side, it's greener where you water it"
- Obscure

All of us are know all about the correlation game, it's that frightful yet habit-forming game where we contrast ourselves and essentially everybody we know and, surprisingly, most awful, all out outsiders. We take a gander at the outer layer of others' lives and however we don't exactly know nor comprehend the entire image of their lives, w rapidly reason that they basically have it better. We analyze ourselves concerning actual traits, material riches, achievements, connections, and the rundown continues endlessly… In the event that we feel that we don't exactly compare our supposed rivalry in at least one of these classifications, we resort to marking ourselves as shameful and unaccomplished also known as "I'm simply bad enough."Admittedly, I also was dependent on this hazardously reckless game.

On my 23rd birthday, I discovered myself feeling a piece discouraged in light of the fact that I felt as though I hadn't accomplished the greater part of what I had set myself to achieve at that point. At the point when somebody dear to me attempted to benevolently comfort me by posting everything that I figured out how to accomplish at the young age of 25 years, I answered "..yet 13-year-olds figured out how to collect sufficient cash to fabricate wells in Africa..and they're around 50% of my age!" To which he replied "Indeed, if that is the way you need to play it, you won't ever win… " thinking back, I understood he was totally correct. At the point when we're so centered around rivaling others and feeling loaded with jealousy of their lives, we wind up living with the deception that we are insufficient except if we keep on taking a stab at flawlessness which doesn't exist, in the first place. The examination game is likewise a ceaseless one since we'll continuously find somebody who we see as more brilliant, more alluring, richer, more cultivated, and so on than ourselves. Actually, each and every one of us is extraordinary and we as a whole have our exceptional reason and way throughout everyday life… Correlation is an outright hoodlum of delight and it keeps us from remembering our good fortune and embracing our generally gorgeous lives. Rather than contrasting our excursion with the excursion of others, we ought to zero in on being appreciative for who are and what we as of now have. main concern is that nobody dominates in the correlation match so we should stop playing this horrendous game unequivocally. Also, assuming you find that you should contend, why not rival yourself? Resolve to apply your work and consideration, every day of the week, to turn out to be preferable over you as of now are and to carry on with your absolute best life. The grass isn't greener on the opposite side, it's greener where you water it. At the point when you direct your concentration and concentration toward turning into your best self, you'll be in wonderment of your development and progress throughout everyday life. Definitely, you'll understand that contrasting yourself with others is only a misuse of precious time and exertion that is obviously better spent zeroing in on your own magnificent life. It will not be even close to a blustery walk around the recreation area however at whatever point you feel that ache of desire or jealousy begins to kick in when you accept that another person has it better than you, center around your excursion all things being equal. Run your race and continue moving towards making YOUR absolute best life. Your future will thank you for it!

Despite the fact that the vast majority of us do whatever it takes not to, all of us in general are to blame of contrasting ourselves with others. We can make examinations like, "I wish I dressed like this and that," or, "I want to be basically as rich as them."

This is much of the time oblivious, however it means a lot to attempt to prepare ourselves to stop. While it might persuade us to better ourselves, continually contrasting ourselves with others can prompt negative considerations.

For what reason do I contrast myself with others?

Individuals are social animals, and correlation is normal all through our whole history.
Virtual entertainment stages like Twitter, Instagram, and Facebook besiege us with posts about what we need. These applications are correlation traps that urge us to address parts of our own lives. It's not difficult to fail to remember that web-based entertainment is a feature reel of others' lives. We see their best minutes, however don't ordinarily observe their battles. We frequently contrast our lesser characteristics and an individual's most desirable characteristics, characteristics our judgment.

How does correlation influence my life?

An excessive amount of correlation prompts despondency and low confidence. We become baffled with ourselves for "not being sufficient," or irate with others.

Some genuine instances of examinations are:

1. You see another lady stroll down the road and think, "I want to be basically as lovely as her."
2. You see a superstar posting on Instagram about their exercise and tell yourself, "If by some stroke of good luck my body seemed to be his."
3. A collaborator is giving a show, and. you can't resist the urge to say, "She's a way preferable public speaker over I am."Feelings of desire, disappointment, and sadness arise in the event that examinations proceed. Assuming left ignored, constant uneasiness and melancholy can originate from such way of behaving.
To stay away from examinations, individuals might search for others' flaws to encourage themselves.
This is similarly all around as unfortunate as destroying yourself for what you don't have or don't resemble.
I need to quit contrasting myself with others: what do I do? To stop the correlation propensity, center around bettering yourself and supporting your certainty. Attempt to prepare your psyche to pull back from ominous examinations. Look for rather to embrace benevolence and an uplifting outlook. It's
difficult work, however it pays off.

Here are a few things you can do to step up to the plate and quit contrasting yourself with others.
1. Know about your triggers and stay away from them to work on your psychological wellness and profound prosperity, rattle off the circumstances and conditions that make you miserable or pessimistic. Virtual entertainment isn't the main thing hurting our confidence. Is there somebody in your life who frequently puts you down? Or on the other hand perhaps you feel insufficient when a partner boasts. Maybe there's a particular place that causes you to feel terrible, such as meandering through a costly store at the shopping center. When you know about circumstances that make you prone to participate in correlations, you can make a move to keep away from them.
2. Limit your experience via web-based entertainment Virtual entertainment stays up with the latest on our loved ones, and recent developments, and brings issues to light. In any case, as

most things, it's best with some restraint. Overlooking via virtual entertainment, particularly while consuming way of life and excellence content, can adversely affect our self-esteem. Unfollow accounts that make you contrast yourself with others. Switch off your telephone following a specific season of day and don't answer each message or remark you get. Inquire as to whether you could invest your energy via virtual entertainment all the more helpfully all things being equal. Might you at any point pursue a book? Take a walk? Call a companion?

3. Try not to look at other people groups' "exterior" to your own "inner parts" Nobody genuinely understands what's going on in the background in another person's life. Everybody is confronting their own struggles

.4. Advise yourself that "cash doesn't purchase joy" There is a connection between psychological well-being and cash. Be that as it may, one thing is valid: cash doesn't purchase bliss. Notwithstanding being barraged with advertisements that say something else, cash doesn't ensure long-lasting joy. Watching superstars carry on with rich ways of life can persuade us to think that cash will tackle our concerns, yet it seldom does. All things considered, it just purchases transitory happiness.

5. Remember your good fortune. Be thankful for what you have. Somebody's life might appear to be better, however there may be someone else out there wishing they had what you had. There's continuously something, even only a certain something, for which you can be grateful. Execute these techniques to adjust your appreciation practice.

6. Use examination as inspiration. Correlations can be an incredible impetus for change, inasmuch as it's solid. Rather than feeling desirous of others' achievements, ponder the way that they had the option to accomplish them. Then, perceive how you can recreate them. Being enlivened by somebody you know to be kinder or more liberal can lead you to be a superior individual.

7. Center around your assets It's alright to be unassuming, yet you ought to likewise be pleased with what you've achieved. An excessive amount of lowliness is similarly essentially as unsafe as a lot of self-assurance. Make a rundown of what you like about yourself. Recording things can help us perceive and acknowledge reality as opposed to talking it resoundingly. You can be as broad or as unambiguous as you like, and let this rundown act as a wake up call of your assets

.8. Celebrate others too We should be our greatest allies, however self-backing can coincide with supporting others. Spread inspiration by giving a shout out to your companions and collaborators for their achievements.

9. Recall that uncertainties are all inclusive. It's typical for you to contrast yourself with others. We as a whole encounter self-questions and fears that outwit us every so often. Indeed, even the most certain individuals feel unreliable at times.

10. Utilize your previous self as a benchmark of examination. The main genuine contest you have is the sort of person you were yesterday, what your identity was last month, or who you were a year prior. You'll have the option to see genuine development through retrospection and be pleased with your development

.Motivating citations to overcome examinations

Here are a few wise words from others that make certain to assist with igniting that desire to quit contrasting

your life to other people and value your astonishing self only a bit more. "Nobody can cause you to feel second rate without your assent." - Eleanor Rosevelt.
"Quit contrasting yourself with others: you are unique. We are unique and it's alright." - Joyce Meyer.B
"I don't maintain that others should conclude what I'm. I need to conclude that for myself." - Emma Watson
"Today you will be you, that is more genuine than valid. There is no one alive who is you-er than you." - Dr.Seuss.

Conclusion

The main individual you ought to contrast yourself with is yourself. Your endeavors ought to zero in on developing from the inside, being kinder, stronger, really buckling down, and being more open rather than whether your hair is sufficiently long or you're essentially major areas of strength for as another person. BetterUp was made to assist us with understanding ourselves and assume responsibility for our own lives. Lucidity, reason, energy, and the apparatuses to pursue what is important to you. BetterUp centers around human change, supporting self-improvement, social associations, and mental wellness, all for the sake of incorporating sound taking care of oneself practices. In the event that you're willing to invest the energy, we're here to guide you through this insane excursion called life.

CHAPTER 5

How The Law Of Correspondence Applies To Business Achievement

What is the Law of Correspondence?

The Law of Correspondence basically made sense that when somebody works on something for you, you feel committed to respond or accomplish something as a trade-off for them. You've probably encountered this in your own life. For example, when you cover the check at lunch for yourself as well as your companion, in the event that they are a decent individual, odds are they'll take care of the check the following time you go out. The vast majority will feel committed and basically deal to do as such. In any case, the Law of Correspondence stretches out past private connections where individuals know one another well. It likewise stretches out to gifts, business, and deals circumstances.

Law of correspondence in real life: helping somebody out and they will help you.

The Law of Correspondence By and by
Do you recollect the Bunny Krishnas? The strict gathering spread its message at air terminals and public social events. Like most strict associations, they had papers that they distributed. They found not many individuals took the papers, gave cash, or paid attention to their message. Until… They started giving gifts. A bloom, a book, a request card… and unexpectedly similar individuals who strolled by them without offering them any consideration were currently halting and giving cash.
Be that as it may, this isn't a peculiarity. Robert Cialdini, the "Guardian of Impact." found that when mints were given with the eatery bill tips went up a normal of 3.1%. The Law of Correspondence likewise works among outsiders. Philip Kunz, a previous social scientist at Brigham Youthful College played out a concentrate in 1974 where he sent Christmas cards to 600 outsiders. He got in excess of 200 answers, some of them up to 4 pages. Also, the correspondence proceeded once the example was started. Kunz got a portion of these yearly Christmas card reactions for as long as 15 years. Individuals feel committed to respond in any event, when they don't have the foggiest idea about the individual starting.
So how might you give the law of correspondence something to do for you?

Utilizing the Law of Correspondence to Expand Business

Assuming you need more interest in your business, you can utilize the Law of Correspondence to get it going. Be that as it may, you should act first (at first). The following are a couple of ways you can do that:
- Post about your involvement in one more business via online entertainment. Label them and let your crowd know the amount you partook in their administration or item. Offer espresso or other free food or drink when potential clients enter your business.
- Give out loot to boost buys. Make tests accessible. Individuals frequently feel committed to purchase subsequent to getting an example.
- Exhibit how well your item chips away at your possible purchasers. At any point stroll by a shopping center booth and somebody attempts to welcome you over to test their lotion? They do this since chances are in the event that you experience the item and like it, you'll purchase basically a little size of the item.
- Give free food to individuals who might actually arrange from you or join forces with you, particularly different organizations. Ask a specialist's office staff how frequently they eat cooked by drug agents. Drug sales reps do it since there's return for capital invested in acquiring lunch.Present somebody as a specialist in their industry and develop them in that capacity. They'll probably give back.
- Offer them consideration and cause them to feel intrigued. Clarify pressing issues and ask their perspective. They'll do likewise for you later on.
- Assume the best about them and the blessing will be gotten back to you.
- Consider a liberal trade strategy. They will esteem your item realizing you esteem them as clients.

- Act incredibly keen to their buys. Besides the fact that it encourages individuals when you value them however they're probably going to purchase more since you show such appreciation for it
- . Contemplate your own life. Who would you like to help? Somebody who doesn't appear to mind when you make a special effort for them or somebody who reliably thank you for your endeavors? The last option, obviously.
- Utilize positive language and a delicate, slow, even tone during client protests. They'll probably quiet their tone to match yours. It's challenging to shout at somebody who's talking compassionate to you with loads of regard.
- Give them a name. Unfortunate way of behaving frequently happens in light of the fact that individuals compartmentalize and don't ponder people around them. For example, I used to work in the lead representative's office handling calls from constituents. I generally realized I was in for a terrible call when it started with "You individuals." On the grounds that while that sounds like the guest saw me personally, they didn't. They had lumped me into the place of government hack, separate from their human life. Furthermore, I realized I needed to restore my humankind in their eyes before they would treat me that way. I needed to assemble sympathy. The equivalent is valid in tending to tables at a smorgasbord. It's simple for coffee shops to fail to remember the tip at a smorgasbord on the off chance that they see the individual looking out for them as a nondescript table busser. Yet, assuming the server gives their name on a rich card, coffee shops before long understand that on the off chance that they don't tip or tip ineffectively, they're doing it to that particular individual.
- Continuously ensure your clients realize they are managing an individual with sentiments and a name. Guaranteeing they realize this will streamline any hardships in the circumstance.
- Offer free classes on the best way to utilize your item. They might purchase an overhaul assuming that they know you're generally there to help it and help them.
- Give counsel regardless of whether it generally benefits you. In the event that they tell the truth about a contender that is luscious, these are there for them, they may not buy from you by then. Yet, they'll recall your genuineness and hope to purchase from you (or suggest you later on) in light of the fact that they trust you and realize you were forthright with them despite the fact that it cost you the deal.
- Offer something for nothing assuming they get it today. Purchasing is many times a profound activity. Normally, the Law of Correspondence expects you to work on something for them first before they'll work on something for you. Be that as it may, once in a while the proposal to do something is sufficient to boost the deal. For example, on the off chance that you offer someone a bonus when they purchase from you they could make it happen. Vehicle sales centers utilize free vehicle washes, oil changes, televisions, or excursions to get individuals to purchase a vehicle. We'll give you this on the off chance that you purchase from us and not the opposition
- Offer free upkeep or checks of your item. On the off chance that you sell an item that requires upkeep, contemplate offering free check-ups. This gives your client genuine serenity yet in addition permits you to propose upsells and extra administrations.

- Remember, you never need to offer things that don't help your client. Assuming you make ideas for upkeep or fixes they needn't bother with, they will feel exploited.
- Have a free evening of fun at your business as a thank you to your dependable clients. They will feel committed to purchase something as long as you don't present the free evening of fun as an infomercial for your item. Try not to be salesy.
- Toss a wine sampling or open house. Once more, individuals will partake in the wine and purchase from you.
- Offer restricted free exhortation. Give clients (restricted) free guidance or free utilization of your administrations. Clarify what they get free of charge and which parts are a paid help. You may be astounded the way that individuals will utilize the free assistance and later update due to correspondence

The tips recorded above fundamentally produce immediate activity by the client or likely client. Be that as it may, a few activities produce long haul results. At the point when you develop credit with your crowd by assisting them with knowing, as, and trust you, you can utilize the Law of Correspondence on another level: a deferred one. This is otherwise called "social capital."

Be an asset and offer all of your insight free of charge. In the end, you'll develop sufficient credit with your crowd that they will do things that you inquire about.

Continuously request some help. You'll be shocked how frequently individuals will accomplish something since you request it. A great many people are not molded to say no. Some might say, "indeed, that depends" and afterward when you uncover how fundamental the blessing is, they'll cheerfully assent.

Request to pay what it's worth. At the point when you give somebody a decent salary or administration and afterward request that they pay what they think it is worth, not very many individuals will pick zero. The Law of Correspondence intends that assuming they find even remote worth in your great or administration, they'll pay something.

If you have any desire to fabricate your business and further develop deals, one of the least demanding ways is to become adroit at the Law of Correspondence. By offering things, information, mastery, guidance, or whatever else, individuals will frequently furnish you with their consideration and cash. There is a sure wizardry to working inside the business and enterprising domains. At the point when you offer something to others you'll ultimately acquire something as a trade off. I'm not discussing credits, or cups of espresso here, however the law of correspondence. This is an unobtrusive yet high level regulation that many expert entrepreneurs know about.

Fascination Versus The Law of Correspondence

Observing the pattern of energy attracting similar energy, you need to have your objective. Then, you want to get your contemplations, sentiments, and activities all in arrangement, pursuing that objective. This, thus, will help you to 'show' or 'draw in' that objective.

And afterward, we have the law of correspondence. So you need to place out something decent into the universe and consequently you'll receive something pleasant consequently. There is a free friendly brain science to this, so we should all continue to dig. Assuming that you are continually attempting to take from the world to get compensated, the world will come searching for you, attempting to get compensated by you consequently! However, on the off chance that you convey valid, genuine worth to the world and everyone around you, treallyreale real worth will likewise get back to you one day. Unexpectedly then something decent you chose to give will track down its direction back to you. This resembles an interest in yourself and is the principal justification for why I accept such a huge amount in bringing genuine, quantifiable worth to my crowd. Be that as it may, as may be obvious, these two regulations have a ton of cross-over.

All along...
You start with an objective. This objective might be a particular kind of way of life, a specific degree of progress, and so forth. Then, you begin utilizing both of these regulations. You get your considerations, sentiments, and activities all in arrangement with this objective, and you begin working for it. You start doing the things most others will not do as you would prefer to the top. As you work for it, you put esteem out into the universe. You improve others' lives. You assist them with tackling their concerns. You spread inspiration, love, delight, and harmony. You become a wellspring of expectation and an incentive for other people. Thus, this covers the two sides of the coin… the pattern of energy attracting similar energy and the law of correspondence. Do both...

Then, you simply keep at it. You continue to do both. You continue living, adjusting your considerations, and making genuine, quantifiable worth. In time, the entirety of this work and great energy will return to you… and you will begin prevailing such that you never even imagined. Recollecting That It Doesn't Generally Return From The Individual You Gave It Toback when I used to sell vehicles, I had this manager who was from Tennessee. He was an esteemed gentleman and a vehicle sales rep… yet he knew a ton about the law of correspondence, and I gleaned some significant knowledge about it working for him. We sold vehicles together, and he was continuously uplifting me to 'give an energy' to specific vehicles on the parcel. We sold a ton of muscle vehicles on the parcel. Speedsters, muscle vehicles, trendy vehicles, and so forth. This' fascinating… .And when things would get slow, he would have me show an adoration and thoughtfulness regarding specific vehicles. For instance… he would agree "That Corvette around there. Show her some consideration." And I would. What's more, sufficiently certain… in a little while, the telephone would ring, and an alternate vehicle would sell. Every so often, he would advise me to go take my lovely sweetheart (presently my better half, Melanie) out for lunch in a specific vehicle. We want to send some activity out," he would agree. "Go feel perfect in that vehicle. We really want something to move." And things would begin to occur...

Furthermore, I would. Furthermore, adequately certain, when I would get back, he would have someone on the line, holding on to buy another vehicle. I knew to the point of realizing that taking that vehicle out, feeling perfect in it, and conveying those uplifting tones were likely not going to make that vehicle sell right at that point. That is Not The way in which It Works
All things being equal, it was more about giving energy out. Going out, cleaning up a vehicle, waxing it, specifying it, taking new pictures of it, tidying up the posting, providing it with that 'feeling' of being cherished.

What's more, adequately certain, something different would click. Something would move, and an alternate vehicle would sell. The law of correspondence picks when and how it compensates you for your energy.

The correspondence meaning we are examining here is a lovely free science. Just endlessly give some more... Then anticipate what returns. You'll be astounded at what comes your direction.

Two Unique Ways Of contemplating Correspondence

There are two distinct ways of contemplating the law of correspondence.

- It is a strategy that you can use to use your work to create more wealth to yourself
- A law of the universe will deal with you if your contemplations, sentiments, and activities adjust to assist you with putting esteem out into the world and make the predetermination you need for yourself.

As may be obvious, these are two altogether different attitudes.

Also, you need to be in accordance with choice 2!

We should continuously think 'esteem first.' NOT 'cash first.'

- Assuming you are satisfied with the consistent concern of getting compensated, you will be wrecking your outlook!

All things being equal, at whatever point you plunk down to compose a blog or make a video, you really want to pose yourself this inquiry. How might I make this substance to do the best on the planet? How might I create this piece of content to help my crowd the most with the issue they are right now confronting?

- In the event that you begin thinking thusly every time you make content, you will begin seeing a Tremendous change in energy in your business!

Believe me. It works for me each and every day. Furthermore, it will work for YOU also one thingthingtaboreciprocityrocity that numerous people don't comprehend is that you can't rush it!

- Assuming you want cash Presently, go get a normal everyday employment and cover your bills that way while you develop esteem with your business.

It took Melanie and me around 4 or 5 years of evenings, ends of the week, and chipping away at our days off to make a critical way of life change with our internet based business. It requires investment.

Yet, assuming that you stay in the right mentality, and don't attempt to rush things, you can make it work.

Fight the temptation to be frantic. Try not to let that appear in your work. All things considered, center around that worth, and take as much time as is needed. Things will occur. Simply continue making and tackling issues.

Conclusion

How you provide for others is undeniably founded on feel. What feels solid in your being? Regardless of whether it's difficult for you to make, it will be gotten with happiness and appreciation by your crowd. As usual, look to offer some benefit first, and watch the profits duplicate

CHAPTER 6

You Don't Need Additional Time, You Simply Have to Spend It Doing What Is important

There's a typical misguided judgment that all that in life comes down to time. Consistently I end up slipping into these equivalent assertions: If by some stroke of good luck I had additional time. I simply need a couple of additional minutes. Two or three hours of work. However it seems like we as a whole are working longer hours without accomplishing more. We accept that all that we need can be accomplished if by some stroke of good luck we had additional time. We erroneously accept that our issues are ones of amount. However Americans as of now work probably the longest hours in the Western World additional time the response is as well?

The Shackles of Opportunity
From our earliest days, we're shown the significance of an everyday construction in view of time. School days are 8 hours in length, with classes organized around openings of time, as opposed to what can be finished. We're instructed that what is important is 'investing the effort', not really completing the work. However to an ever increasing extent, we're creating some distance from this standard practice.
An ever increasing number of individuals are working from a distance, or in non-standard ways as seasonal workers, workers for hire, or shift laborers. The 8-hour day has been pushed out. In any case, is this the delivery from the design that we trusted it could be? The opportunity to take care of our responsibilities at whatever point apparently gives us the opportunity to make our timetable — whether that implies 9-5, 7-2, 2-10, 1-4, or whatever seems best for you. It likewise implies we're allowed to spend so a lot (or a brief period) filling in as long as the gig gets wrapped up. However, research shows that those with the opportunity to work less, wind up working essentially more.

A thorough report on hours worked and efficiency by the Global Work Association found that the normal specialist who had the opportunity to set their hours worked 54 hours of the week, versus 37 hours seven days by those with set plans. That is an additional 17 working hours seven days, just from the 'opportunity' to pick your hours. Much more dreadful, those additional hours don't prompt quality, useful work.

At the point when the Association for Monetary Collaboration and Improvement took a gander at the impact of extended periods on efficiency in 18 European nations over a 66 year period, our per-hour efficiency during an expansion in working time generally reduces. That, the profits reduce all the more quickly for longer working times. The more we work, the less proficient we become. What's more, when we pass a specific limit it just deteriorates.

And that implies more hours went through working the following day to make up for lost time and fix the errors we've made. And that implies more hours worked altogether. And that implies even lower efficiency. Without any end in sight and on. So for what reason do we make it happen? I realize we've all confronted those minutes where we feel dull yet keep on trudging through the work, just to retry a large portion of it when we're new and rested. Perhaps it's pride. Or on the other hand a feeling of obligation. One response, which appears to sound good to me, is Parkinson's Law:Work grows to occupy the time accessible for its completion."This 'regulation' was begat by Cyril Northcote Parkinson as a feature of an entertaining paper in The Financial specialist. As one model, Parkinson makes sense of how:An old woman of recreation can go through the whole day composing and despatching a postcard to her niece at Bognor Regis. An hour will be spent in tracking down the postcard, one more in chasing after exhibitions, thirty minutes in a quest for the location, an hour and a quarter in synthesis, and twenty minutes in choosing whether or not to take an umbrella while going to the support point close to the following road. The all out exertion which would possess a bustling person for three minutes generally told may in this mold leave someone else's prostate following a day of uncertainty, uneasiness, and toil."The additional time we give an errand, the additional time we spend on it. Furthermore, the additional time we spend on an errand, the more regrettable of a task we do.

We can't fire on all chambers for quite a long time at a time. Inspiration, resolve, and center are undeniably restricted assets that we want to utilize sparingly over the course of the day. Investing more energy just kills inspiration and debilitates the work we're doing. So assuming we work less, we'll be more joyful and more useful?

I've generally felt that I simply needed more opportunity to see companions, keep up connections, and do my desired things that would keep me cheerful. Despite the fact that investing energy with my loved ones is one of my central individual qualities, I actually considered the issue to be one of money. I simply needed more opportunity to make everything work. Stirring less opens up additional opportunities for mingling and doing things that assist with our prosperity. Sounds great, right? Invest less energy working and possess more energy for relaxation and chatting with the ones we love. However it doesn't exactly work that way.

What was amazing was that the concentrate additionally tracked down this equivalent example in jobless individuals. Indeed, even those without the prerequisite to be some place during the week were less blissful during the week of work. Youthful and Lim attach this to organize great — that associating with others is more significant for our prosperity than simply uninterrupted alone time. You basically can't get more ends of the week's by simply going home for the day yourself.

Decide to Set aside a few minutes for the Work That Is important

So we can't work more hours to be better at our specific employment, and we can't invest more energy off to be more joyful. So what decision do we have? The objective is to zero in on effectiveness, as opposed to yield. There's a snare we fall into legitimizing the work when assets put in. "I've burned through 60 hours/4 months/8 years on this. I merit it to be a triumph." The cutting edge working environment maxim is that it's really not necessary to focus on the hours, it's about the work. However for the vast majority telecommuters or those functioning non-standard hours, this implies fruition regardless of the expense. However, to celebrate spending X measure of hours on an undertaking versus 10X that time is crazy. Assuming that we're to gauge just what finishes, nullifying the setting of how long it is required to get done with the job and how effective somebodyis, we're feeling the loss of the entire picture. Efficiency isn't just about what you finish. It's the way effective you are at getting those errands finished. A new report by Julian Birkinshaw of the London Institute of Business found that most information laborers, designers, essayists, and the individuals who 'think professionally' — spend on normal 41% of their experience on positions we could without much of a stretch give to other people. Naturally, we stick to undertakings that keep us 'occupied' (and along these lines, significant). We feel better with a full timetable and an escape prison free card for all of our life obligations. Strangely, as we as a whole make progress toward additional time, we clutch the things that take up most within recent memory. So vanity, once more, is an explanation we lose efficiency. The need to seem occupied and significant. However, pursuing turning out to be more effective is unimaginably difficult to follow. Forthright interest in abilities, arranging, or preparing others to take over consistently prompts long haul proficiency, opening up the time you have for the work that is important. Not the bustling errands.

Rethinking How We Work and Live

In all parts of our lives — whether it's work or individual — amount is seldom the issue. Time spent working is a vanity metric. Also, uninterrupted alone time without associating with loved ones is practically unimportant. The issue of amount is one we can't change. It simply is absolutely impossible to get additional opportunities in your day. What's more, the compound impacts of working extended periods and late evenings imply that you generally emerge on the base. So it's a question of value. Productivity. Picking how long to spend functioning and choosing what's the most ideal way to invest that energy. At the point when we pick, we quit considering time the main estimation of our day.

The following are a couple of ways of assisting you with picking how to invest your energy that surfaced during my examination for this article. Everyone can be utilized as a channel to conclude regardless of whether you're working effectively.

Plan for Assignments, Not Time

In his exposition on creator time versus supervisor time, writer Paul Graham recommends that specialists, for example, essayists and software engineers work in units of a portion of a day in any event, as opposed to the hourly or half-hourly lumps of a director's timetable. By and by, the best work I do comes when the undertakings that I need don't need a severe course of events or timetable. Perusing, composing, altering... These turn out best for me when I don't need to stretch or stress to squeeze into the portion on my timetable. Working an errand to the end provides you with an estimation of progress — something you can use to reply: am I working proficiently?

At the point when You Find Worth, Continue To work

Inspiration and energy are restricted assets, and squandering them ruins our possibilities of finishing significant work. In Dr. Steel's investigations on delaying and inspiration, he observed that worth is one of the main parts of keeping up with our inspiration. At the point when the work we're doing has worth to us, we're more persuaded to work. Why stop? Gatherings can be pushed, yet streams won't be quickly recreated.

Center around Being Better, Quicker, More grounded

As Henry David Thoreau composed:
"It isn't sufficient to be occupied. The subterranean insects are as well. The inquiry is: What are we occupied with?"
As inventive business mentor Imprint McGuiness makes sense of, we really want to zero in on something major every day that will cause us to feel accomplished. Try not to sit at your work area just to be there and congratulate yourself. Center around finishing your day's worth of effort and having a decent outlook on it. Then leave. The main way we can change how we work is by adjusting our attitude about how we work

Request Help

Generally we get so enveloped with occupied work that we fail to remember we can request help. Particularly in little groups where you realize everybody's plate is full, venturing into another person's business day and intruding on them is one that a couple of us need to do. However, that speedy inquiry or short discussion could be the contrast between spending an hour or 5 minutes on an undertaking.NUtilize the information on individuals around you so that when you take care of business, you work productively. You don't require additional time. You really want a superior time. Also, that main comes through moving toward your work and existence with the comprehension that extended periods spent working accomplish great work.

As Seth Godin so suitably puts it: "You don't require additional time... you simply have to decide." Time is quite often an issue of value, not amount. So settle on what is important, and afterward make it happen.
You don't require additional time

CHAPTER 7

KNOW YOURSELF

To realize yourself totally is to have encountered being with God and to approach at any second to reality this colossal experience uncovers. The experience gives the constant conviction of being answerable for each snapshot of your life: that whatever occurs, the upside, the awful, and the impassive, is your own will. Inside this all-supporting information is the obvious assurance of everlasting status and yet, it is additionally conceivable to encounter liability regarding the quick climate lastly for the whole universe including the world's evident disunity of war and languishing. experience reality and insight than the experience of being alive. However, you should not trust me. You should acknowledge it in yourself, know It, as far as it might be concerned, is beyond anything that can be described and thought of. Also, it must be capable without a plan of action to medications or madness. Then, at that point, you should experience

your insight; be your insight. Truth is for all people, not only for yourself.

Building your Inside Emotionally supportive network

To fabricate an underpinning of help for our excursion, we will need to distinguish the various ways we can assist ourselves with having a real sense of reassurance and security en route. Not even one of us has some control over our general surroundings, so supporting us to make a space inside ourselves permits us to answer the world in sound ways. I like to consider our interior emotionally supportive network a device the crate we can access whenever, particularly to assist us with getting past troublesome or unpleasant
feelings.

Here Are A few Instances of Utilizing Inner Help

- You discover yourself feeling very restless and can't put your finger on why. You choose to go on a speedy, lively fifteen-minute stroll around your area. You notice your feelings and contemplations shift and you're feeling a piece more settled when you return home.
- You awakened feeling miserable and just can't track down the inspiration to do anything on your plan for the day. You sit on your bed and conclude that you will do a five-minute breathing method. You notice you feel less resentful and can do a fast errand that you've been putting off. After an extreme discussion with your accomplice, you feel overpowered and notice some outrage coming up. You do a straightforward establishing exercise, seeing the varieties in the room and the manner in which the ground upholds your body. A short time later, you notice you separated the pattern of meddlesome contemplations and feel
somewhat less fomented. You then get your diary to communicate some of what you're feeling to assist with handling your other feelings.
- The entire day you've felt off. You notice that you've been condemning and making a decision about yourself over the course of the day so as sunset comes, you focus on getting into bed early. Extra time, you've seen that you will more often than not feel as such when you want rest and give yourself the rest you really want to start a new
day tomorrow.

Making A Feeling that everything is safe and secure

Wellbeing and security are basic to this mending excursion of self-disclosure. Utilizing the instruments beneath will assist you with building a groundwork of internal wellbeing you can access whenever. At the point when we don't have a real sense of reassurance due to the ongoing conditions, or as a result of injury that keeps on living in our bodies, we can't hear the pings from our true Selves. Reliably getting to this place of refuge inside will help you reconnect with this most profound piece of you. Keep in mind, it's not just alright to enjoy reprieves, it's critical to do as such. The more you practice, the more agreeable you'll become with the different awkward impressions that might emerge with this work.Utilize Your Breath to Make Security Figuring out how to utilize our breath is a strong method for managing our sensory system. At the point when we experience pressure, our breathing becomes shallow and fast. Here and there, we could wind up pausing our breathing and holding our jaws. These physiological movements send our body a message that we are undependable, and that now is the right time to plan for a danger. By figuring out how to purposefully have an impact on the manner in which we inhale, we can show our bodies that we are protected. Here are a portion of my breathing activities.

Make a Tactile Encounter

Utilizing your faculties assists with establishing you, or to move your consideration away from your reasoning brain to what's going on in your body or your environmental factors. This can be extraordinarily useful when your contemplations are causing pressure or close to home overpower. Utilizing the rundown beneath, pick one action to rehearse this tactile establishing exercise. In the wake of putting in almost no time reconnecting with your faculties, check in with how your body feels. Light a candle and put it on shortly just watching its fire. Consume some

incense and put in no time flat smelling its fragrance. Get a cut of orange or other delicious leafy foods a couple of seconds as you gradually gnaw on its new delectable juices. View as your pet or a most loved cover and put in no time flat scouring your hand over its delicateness. Put on your number one music and spend a few seconds paying attention to the sounds and tunes. Find Your Ground Drawing in with nature is a strong method for quieting a focus on the body. At the point when you put in almost no time reconnecting with the earth underneath you, the sights and hints of the nature around you, or the sun above you, your
stress chemicals start to diminish, assisting you with feeling a piece more secure.

Reconnect to the Earth
• Carry your regard for your feet and notice how the impact point and underside of the two feet connect with the ground. Take your shoes off (if workable) for additional contact with the earth. Burn through two to five minutes simply feeling the ground under you.
• Encircle yourself with nature by sitting in a nursery or a nearby park, or visiting your plant subterranean insects burning through two to five minutes completely encountering the nature around you.
• Stand in the daylight and spotlight your strain on the sensation of its glow on your skin.

Nature mend
Research reliably shows that being encircled naturally for just twenty minutes can bring down pressure chemicals. In any event, being in the sun for a couple of moments can assist with expanding serotonin and dopamine, synthetic compounds that assume a part in our sensations of prosperity. Find the closest park, climbing trail, or even a spot in your terrace, or sit outside on the following radiant day and notice the
impacts of investing this energy outside.

Imagine Wellbeing and Unwinding
Sit down, or set down, in an agreeable
space where you can securely unwind and ' will not be intruded. Shut your eyes (in the event that it has a good sense of reassurance to do as such) and concentrate on relaxing. Start to picture a white, sparkling light around your heart. As you keep on breathing profoundly envision the white light becoming more grounded and feeling your heart relaxing and opening simultaneously. As you feel more loose, imagine the white light fill-in the whole region of your chest and rehash
out loud or quietly to yourself: "My heart is protected. I'm protected. I'm open and free."
Following your spending routinely can provide you with a precise picture of where your cash is going — and where you'd like it to go all things being equal. Then, at that point, by utilizing a spending plan, you can precisely represent every one of the bills you really want to pay proceeding. However, before you begin connecting numbers to a bookkeeping sheet or application, require a moment to rattle off every one of your month to month expenses.
This is the way to begin following your month to month expenses.

Actually take a look at your record proclamations

Pinpoint your cash propensities by taking stock of your records in general, including your financial records and all Visas you have. Taking a gander at your records will assist you with distinguishing your spending designs. Your spending will comprise of both fixed costs and variable costs. Fixed costs are more averse to change from one month to another. They incorporate home loan or lease, utilities, protection, and obligation installments. You'll have more space to change variable costs like food, dress, and travel

Arrange your costs
Start by gathering your costs. Some individual accounting sites and charge cards naturally label your buys in classifications like "retail chain" or "car." You could find that spur of the moment purchases at Target are setting you back a great deal. Or on the other hand perhaps you'll understand you're for repeating membership benefits that you could manage without. Then, at that point, arranging those costs into requirements and needs can assist you with sorting out your financial plan and focus on spending, particularly assuming you want to manage expenses to account for reserve funds or obligation reimbursement.

Needs
These are the costs you can't keep away from. Assuming you utilize the 50/30/20 financial plan, these ought to represent half of your spending. Necessities frequently incorporate the accompanying:
- Lodging: Home loan or lease; property holders or tenants protection; local charge (while perhaps not currently in the home loan installment).
- Transportation: Vehicle installment, gas, upkeep, and accident coverage; public transportation.
- Medical care: Health care coverage; personal clinical expenses.
- Disaster protection
- Utilities: Power and petroleum gas; water; disinfection/trash; web; phone as well as landline. Food, toiletries and hair styles, and different fundamentals.
- Kid care.
- Understudy loan installments; other least advance installments; kid backing or provision installments.

Wants
These expenses may be harder to account for in a budget, as they don't always come with a set monthly fee. If you use the 50/30/20 budget, wants can account for up to 30% of your spending.
- Clothing, jewelry, etc.
- Dining out, special meals in (steaks for the grill, etc.).
- Alcohol.
- Movie, concert, and event tickets.
- Gym or club memberships.
- Travel expenses (airline tickets, hotels, rental cars, etc.)
- Cable or streaming packages.
- Self-care treats like spa visits and pedicures.
- Home decor.Savings and debt repayment

This is the money you're putting toward your retirement, emergency fund, and other savings, and using to pay down high-interest credit cards and other "toxic" debt like payday loans. It also for your "great obligations, for example, your understudy loans and home loan. In the 50/30/20 financial plan, this ought to represent 20% of your pay.
- Just-in-case account.
- Bank account.
- Individual retirement account.
- Different ventures.
- Charge card installments (see financial plan tip beneath).
- Additional installments on the home loan.
- Additional installments on educational loans

.Construct your spending plan
Include your costs for every classification of necessities, needs, and reserve funds/obligations, then plug in your month to month net gain underneath. At regular intervals, return to your spending plan and change as needs be. Consider utilizing a spending plan application to follow your uses, saving time as you gather speed with your new planning propensity. Assuming you stall out, attempt these planning tips. Planning or cost following applications Planning applications like You Really want a Spending plan and Mint are intended for in a hurry cash the executives, allowing you to dispense a specific measure of spendable pay every month relying upon what you're taking in and what you're paying out. These sorts of applications will work in the event that you're willing to log your purchases, set forth the effort, and adhere to your spending plan. Contingent upon what you receive in return, a paid application might merit the expense. You Want a Spending plan, for example, is $99 per year or $14.99 per month (following a 34-day free preliminary), yet it has engaging advantages, similar to its capacity to match up exchanges straightforwardly from your financial balance and its choice for live studios with the organization's help group. NerdWallet has likewise distinguished the best cost following applications in view of evaluations and prominence among clients.
.

Investigate other cost trackers
Not a devotee of applications? A calculation sheet is another significant cash following device. You can find an assortment of free financial plan layouts on the web, and NerdWallet likewise offers an internet based financial plan worksheet.
Or on the other hand, in the event that you have what is happening, for example, speculations or a business, you should seriously mull over Revive, which allows you to import bank exchanges and screen your ventures.
Revive offers work area programming with broad planning and following highlights and furthermore has a versatile instrument: the Simplifi planning application. Memberships are charged yearly and normal month to month costs for the work area programming range from $3.49 for the "starter" rendition to $8.99 for the home and business releases.

Distinguish space for change
As you track, be prepared to adapt. Bringing down the huge fixed costs in your day to day existence, similar to the expense of lodging, vehicle u andutilitiestimeses can have a massive

effect on your spending plan. Past that, look at extra cash saving tips that can give you some space to breathe and need geeky information that is customized to your cash.
Bring all your cash into one view, and get fitted experiences to take full advantage of it. Find out more.

Investigate what you own — and what you owe.
You might claim a vehicle or a home — or have cash in the bank. Put it all together, and it can appear to be significant. Yet, to genuinely understand what you own, you need to figure out what you owe. The blend of what you own (your resources) and what you owe (your liabilities) makes up your total assets. Realizing your total assets is significant for two reasons:

- It allows you to grasp what is going on.
- It gives you a reference point for estimating progress toward your objectives.

In a perfect world, as you proceed to procure and save, your total assets will develop. Assuming your total assets are low or bleeding cash, you'll have to deal with saving more and spending less. To watch your advancement, compute your total assets now and recalculate it more than once per year.

Step by step instructions to set up an individual total assets proclamation.
Setting up a total assets proclamation is pretty much as simple as making a straightforward agenda and doing some fundamental math.

1. List your resources (what you own), gauge the worth of each, and include the aggregate. Incorporate things, for example,
    - Cash in your ledgers
    - Worth of your speculation accounts
    - Your vehicle
    - The market worth of your home
    - Financial matters
    - Individual property, like gems, workmanship, and furniture
    - Cash worth of any insurance contracts

2. List your liabilities (what you owe) and include the extraordinary equilibriums. Incorporate things, for example,
    - Contract
    - Vehicle credit
    - Mastercard balance
    - Understudy loans

3. Deduct your liabilities from your resources to decide your total assets.
Need assistance ascertaining? Figure out your total assets rapidly and effectively with our total assets worksheet

Why following your costs is critical to becoming rich

One of the keys to creating financial wellbeing is taking care of your cash shrewdly. On the off chance that you don't have the best cash the board abilities, then, at that point, regardless of whether you in the end become rich, you probably won't remain rich for a really long time. What's more, the groundwork of good cash the executives is having the option to follow your spending.

Following your spending has a few advantages. To begin with, it can provide you with a reasonable thought of precisely where your cash is going every month. At the point when you don't watch out for your costs, it's not difficult to overspend without acknowledging it. For example, the typical American spends around $483 each month on trivial expenses, despite the fact that near 60% of those equivalent individuals say they're living check to check, a review from Charles Schwab found. On the off chance that you don't know precisely the amount you're spending every month and where your cash is going, it can feel like you're attempting to scrape by monetarily - - regardless of whether you have a lot of money in excess.

One more advantage of following your cash is that it makes it simpler to check whether there are regions of your financial plan where you can scale back. At times it's difficult to get a handle on precisely the amount you're spending on specific costs, particularly more modest expenses. Assuming you go through $10 each day venturing out on a brief siesta, that doesn't seem like it would have a massive effect on your generally speaking monetary circumstance. Yet, that $10 each day can transform into $300 each month or $3,600 each year. At the point when you have every one of your costs delineated before you, it's simpler to recognize these patterns and cut back assuming your ways of managing money begin to gain out of influence.

Develop reserve funds dramatically by financial planning
Yet, finding additional cash in your financial plan is just the principal half of the situation with regards to creating financial wellbeing. You additionally need to put away your cash shrewdly if you have any desire to expand it. Presently, that doesn't mean you ought to toss every one of your investment funds into a solitary remarkable new stock you think will be the following huge thing. Rather, a gradual methodology can help you reliably (and securely) create financial momentum after some time. One of the most mind-blowing ways of procuring somewhat high paces of return while restricting your gamble is to put resources into minimal expense record reserves and common assets, which are enormous assortments of stocks, bonds, and different protections. One of the most engaging elements of these assets is that you can expand your ventures. So instead of placing all your cash into a couple of individual stocks, you're spreading your money across handfuls or even many various ventures. Albeit that might sound complex, getting everything rolling putting resources into these kinds of funds is simple. On the off chance that you're saving in a 401(k) or IRA, you're most likely previously putting resources into the record and shared reserves. Obviously, similar to any speculation, record reserves and shared reserves don't necessarily in every case see positive returns. There will be highs and lows, however given sufficient opportunity, you ought to see your cash develop dramatically. Furthermore, regardless of whether you have a lot to save every month, the additional time you need to allow your speculations to compound, the more extravagant you'll be. For instance, suppose you've begun following your costs and found that you can cut your spending by around $200 each month. In the event that you put away that cash and are procuring a 7% yearly pace

of return, you'll collect nearly $152,000 in the next 25 years. On the off chance that you're ready to bury, say, $300 each month, your reserve funds will move to around $228,000 in a similar period.

Slow yet consistent comes out on top in the cash race
Following your costs and contributing your reserve funds isn't an easy money scam, and you will not turn into a mogul short-term. In any case, you will wind up more extravagant than you are presently, and contingent upon the amount you're ready to store every month and how long you need to save, you could wind up accumulating more than $1 million. NoBuilding abundance takes time, however it's an attainable objective. Also, best of all, it requires negligible work to begin saving at this point. You can either follow your costs as it was done in the good 'ol days by keeping your receipts and building a calculation sheet, or you can adopt a more current strategy by matching up your financial balances and charge cards to an application that accomplishes basically everything for you.

Despite what strategy you pick, following your spending is vital to building sound monetary propensities. When you have a decent comprehension of what you're spending as opposed to saving every month, it becomes simpler to scale back, save more, and create financial momentum each dollar in turn.

CHAPTER 8

Wealth:true importance of riches

What Is Abundance?

Abundance estimates the worth of the relative multitude of resources of worth possessed by an individual, local area, organization, or country. Not entirely set in stone by taking the all out market worth of all physical and elusive resources possessed, then deducting all obligations. Basically, abundance is the amassing of scant assets. Explicit individuals, associations, and countries are supposed to be well off when they can collect numerous significant assets or merchandise. Abundance can be differentiated to pay in that abundance is a stock and pay is a stream, and it very well may be seen in one or the other outright or relative terms

Grasping Abundance
Abundance can be communicated in different ways. In a simply material sense, abundance comprises the multitude of genuine assets under one's influence. Monetarily, total assets is the most well-known articulation of abundance. Definitions and proportions of abundance have been different over the long run among social orders. In current culture, cash is the most well-known method for estimating abundance. Estimating abundance in terms of cash is an illustration of cash's capability as a unit of record. The degree to which outside powers can

control the worth of cash can decisively affect estimating abundance along these lines, however it gives a helpful shared factor to examination. Any other way, land and even animals can be utilized to gauge and assess abundance. The antiquated Egyptians, for example, when estimated abundance in light of wheat. Crowding societies have frequently utilized sheep, ponies, or cows as proportions of abundance.

Step by step instructions to Gauge Riches
Estimating abundance as far as cash conquers the issue of assessing abundance as various types of merchandise. These qualities can then be added or deducted together. This, thus, allows the helpful utilization of total assets as a proportion of riches. Total assets is equivalent to resources less liabilities. For organizations, total assets is otherwise called investor's value or book esteem. In like manner sense terms, total assets communicate abundance as every one of the genuine assets under one's influence, barring those that eventually have a place with another person. Abundance is a stock variable, rather than a stream variable like pay. Abundance estimates how much important monetary merchandise that has been gathered at a given moment; pay estimates how much cash (or products) that has gotten over a given time period. Pay addresses the expansion to abundance over the long haul (or deduction, assuming it is negative). An individual whose total compensation is positive over the long run will turn out to be progressively rich over the long haul. For nations, GDP (Gross domestic product) can be considered a proportion of pay (a stream variable), however it is frequently wrongly alluded to as a proportion of riches (a stock variable).

Any individual who has collected a huge amount of total assets can be viewed as rich, however the vast majority consider this term in even more a relative sense. Whether estimated as far as cash and total assets or items like wheat or sheep, all out abundance can fluctuate among people and gatherings. The overall distinctions in abundance between individuals are what we generally allude to characterize who is rich or not. Research has reliably shown that individuals' view of their prosperity and joy depends considerably more on their assessments of abundance comparative with others than on outright riches. This is additionally essential for why the idea of abundance is typically applied exclusively to scant financial products; merchandise that are plentiful and free for everybody give no premise to relative examinations across people.

History
Adam Smith, in his original work The Abundance of Countries, depicted abundance as "the yearly produce of the land and work of the general public". This "produce" is, at its most straightforward, a decent or administration which fulfills human requirements, and needs of utility.

In famous utilization, abundance can be depicted as an overflow of things of financial worth, or the condition of controlling or having such things, typically as cash, land, and individual property. A person who is viewed as well off, prosperous, or rich is somebody who has aggregated significant abundance comparative with others in their general public or reference bunch.

In financial matters, total assets alludes to the worth of resources claimed short of the worth of liabilities owed at a point in time. Abundance can be classified into three head classifications: individual property, including homes or vehicles; money related reserve funds, for example, the collection of past and man made production including land, stocks, securities, and organizations. This multitude of depictions make abundance a particularly significant piece of social delineation. Abundance gives a kind of individual wellbeing net of security against an unexpected decrease in one's expectation for everyday comforts in case of employment cutback or different crises and can be changed into house buying, business proprietorship, or even an advanced degree by extending the abundance to finish an acquisition of such.

Abundance has been characterized as an assortment of things restricted in supply, adaptable, and helpful in fulfilling human desires. Shortage is a basic calculus of riches. At the point when an attractive or significant item (adaptable, great or expertise) is bountiful to everybody, the proprietor of the ware will have no potential for riches. At the point when a significant or positive product is in scant stock, the proprietor of the ware will have extraordinary potential for riches.

'Abundance' alludes to some amassing of assets (net resource esteem), regardless of whether it is bountiful. 'Lavishness' alludes to an overflow of such assets (pay or stream). A well off individual, local area, or country hence has more collected assets (capital) than an unfortunate one. Something contrary to abundance is desperation. Something contrary to extravagance is neediness.

The term suggests a common agreement on laying out and keeping up with responsibility for things which can be summoned with practically zero exertion and cost with respect to the proprietor. The idea of abundance is relative and shifts between social orders as well as fluctuates between various areas or locales in a similar society. An individual total assets of US$10,000 in many pieces of the US would positively not place an individual among the richest residents of that district. Be that as it may, such a sum would comprise a remarkable measure of abundance in ruined non-industrial nations.

Ideas of abundance additionally fluctuate across time. Current work saving creations and the advancement of the sciences have immensely worked on the way of life in present day cultures for even the most unfortunate of individuals. This similar abundance across time is additionally material to what was to come; considering this pattern of human headway, the way of life that the richest appreciate today might be viewed as ruined by people in the future.

Industrialization stressed the job of innovation. Many positions were mechanized. Machines supplanted some worworkers'ilandererrkerer on the grounds that specialize on labor that are basic on monetary achievement However, actual capital, as it came to be known, comprising of both normal capital and infrastructural capital, turned into the focal point of the investigation of wealth.[citation needed]
Adam Smith considered abundance creation to be the blend of materials, work, land, and innovation so as to catch a benefit (overabundance over the expense of production) The hypotheses of David Ricardo, John Locke, and John Stuart Factory, in the eighteenth hundred

years and nineteenth hundreds of years based on these perspectives on abundance that we presently call traditional financial matters. Marxian financial matters (see work hypothesis of significant worth) recognizes in the Grundrisse between material abundance and human riches, characterizing human abundance as "abundance in human relations"; land and work were the wellsprings of all material riches. The German social student of history Silvio Vietta joins abundance/neediness to objectivity. Having a main situation in the improvement of objective sciences, new technologies,s and financial products, while the inverse can be connected with poverty.

Measure of abundance on the planet
The abundance of families overall adds up to US$280 trillion (2017). As per the eighth release of the Worldwide Abundance Report, in the year to mid-2017, complete worldwide abundance increased at a pace of 6.4%, the quickest pace beginning around 2012, and arrived at US$280 trillion, an increase of US$16.7 trillion. This reflected far and wide gains in value markets matched by comparable ascents in non-monetary resources, which moved over the pre-emergency year 2007's level interestingly this year. Abundance development likewise outperformed populace development, with the goal that worldwide mean abundance per grown-up developed by 4.9% and arrived at another record high of US$56,540 per grown-up. Tim Harford has stated that a little youngster has more prominent abundance than the 2 billion least fortunate individuals on the planet consolidated since a little kid has no obligation.

As per the 2021 worldwide abundance report by McKinsey and Company, the overall all out total assets is presently at US$514 trillion of every 2020, with China being the richest country with a total assets of US$120 trillion. In any case, one more report by Credit Suisse in 2021 found that the absolute abundance of the US actually surpassed that of China, with the US having US$126.3 trillion and China having US$74.9 trillion

CHAPTER 9

There is continuously a new thing to learn

The act of learning will assist you with grasping yourself and your general surroundings. At the point when you find out about yourself, you work on your capacity to impart your necessities, put down clear stopping points, and pursue choices for your life and vocation. What's more, when you extend how you might interpret the world, you interface yourself to the worldwide local area. You figure out how to add to individuals' lives at home and at work. Advancing likewise makes you a more versatile individual — an expertise that is vigorously esteemed by businesses. It means a lot to stay aware of industry patterns, get new abilities, and foster more effective work processes. These things will help your profession and work on your worth to your group. What's more, assuming you actually need motivation to continue learning, research shows that learning improves your personal satisfaction. There are even a few emotional wellness benefits related with figuring out how to learn:

- Decreased pressure
- Worked on fearlessness
- Expanded information
- Worked on mental prosperity
- Expanded chances to construct social association

Additionally, it's good times! Life's more energetic when you really try to discover some new information consistently.

Individuals can be visual, physical, or hear-able students. You could appreciate paying attention to book recordings, working with your hands, or watching a narrative. Whatever your style, it's valuable to follow a learning pathway, which is a psyche map that keeps tabs on your development on your objectives. At BetterUp, we can assist you on your learning with venturing. Our mentors champion individual prosperity and development, social associations, and initiative and vocation advancement. What better method for rolling out an enduring improvement than by learning?

5 moves toward develop the propensity for learning
Fruitful people are devoted to long lasting opportunities for growth. You don't have to go to a top college to figure out how to be a decent understudy, all things considered. As a matter of fact, the way to being a long lasting student is to take an expansive perspective on learning. Notice, we didn't call it instruction or school? With interest and a development outlook, gaining some new useful knowledge consistently is beyond difficult not. That being said, more purposeful, coordinated learning is fulfilling and useful.

The following are five moves toward assist you with developing this propensity:

1. Figure out what you need to be aware
There's a distinction between cherishing something and picking up something. Whenever you find a part of your life where you need information or distinguish an expertise you might want to improve, record it on paper. Monitor things you feel propelled to find out about. At the point when you begin taking a gander at the world from the perspective of these areas you need to find out about, you'll track down bunches of chances to learn.

2. Put forth objectives
Having objectives allows you to plan and do whatever it may take to begin getting the right stuff you want. The human mind can unfortunately hold a limited amount much immediately. Rather

than attempting to learn everything rapidly, begin with microlearning or presenting yourself to data in scaled down pieces. Perusing a couple of news stories or standing by listening to a short web recording every morning is an extraordinary method for engrossing pieces of data every day.

3. Utilize numerous mediums
Our reality is more interconnected than any time in recent memory. You can get to numerous assets on the web: classes, digital broadcasts, books, TED talks, and that's just the beginning. Blend and match how you figure out how to improve your data ingestion. It'll keep you invigorated and things intriguing.

4. Put learning into your timetable
Picking a movement to learn is a certain something, however it is one more to have conviction. On the off chance that you don't carve out opportunity to learn, you will not move along. Any measure of time is not the best, but not terrible either than nothing.

5. Encircle yourself with different students
Are individuals you spend time with pushing you to improve or be more gutsy? Might you at any point discuss various subjects with them, or would they say they are unsupportive? Others impact our propensities. Investing energy with positive people who are similarly however inquisitive as we may be will give you that additional push to proceed with in any event, when you're disappointed. You can likewise gain from each other. Share with them what you've realized for the current week in your perusing or tuning in, and they could share right back. Following individuals who are specialists at what you're realizing via virtual entertainment will assist with expanding the positive energy around you, as well. Keep in mind: everybody you meet knows something that you don't. Assuming that you're available to gaining from them, they'll open to share.

What amount of time does it require to learn something?
Overall, shaping another propensity requires 66 days. In any case, actually an opportunity to foster another propensity changes — all things considered, a few propensities are simpler to create than others. That is valid for dominating abilities, as well. In any case, you needn't bother with to be a specialist to appreciate something or excel. Contemplate your expert objectives, as well. Businesses need balanced laborers. They additionally need laborers who can upskill themselves and keep awake to-date on changes in the field. Enduring a year mastering a solitary expertise isn't the most proficient methodology in the event that your center is supporting your profession. In the event that you're gaining some new useful knowledge since you have an energetic outlook on it, the time span might be less significant. Learning new things requires tolerance and determination, yet knowing how you learn best will assist the cycle with going faster.

The most effective method to gain some new useful knowledge
It doesn't make any difference what sort of student you are; numerous assets are accessible to assist with showing you another ability. The following are seven methods for doing that.

1. Practice speed perusing
This is a mastering expertise that works on your visual framework and maintenance. On account of speed perusing, you will assimilate and review data faster over the long haul.

2. Visit web based learning destinations
Learning doesn't need to be formal or organized, however at times we really want essential information. Also, now and then we want design to keep us persuaded. Online courses can connect customary schooling and independent learning.

3. Treat botches as data, not disappointment
Botches are our best instructors. In the event that you don't commit errors, you will not improve, and thinking about what happened gives you the skill to improve sometime later.

4. Get inquisitive (and befriend your internal identity)
The interest of kids is something enchanted. They're keen on everything. Investigate the new, the abnormal, and the difficult. Keep in mind, while you're realizing, there are no moronic inquiries.

5. Get physical
Learning is a psychological cycle, and our psychological wellbeing benefits from active work. Expanding your pulse implies that more oxygen goes to your cerebrum. This thusly reinforces your concentration and advances cerebrum versatility. Cerebrum versatility alludes to the brain associations that assist us with acquiring abilities.

6. Telephone a companion
Learning is more enjoyable with a mate. Having somebody to go to for help pushes us along. Request that companions go along with you in learning-related attempts to assist with considering each other responsible. You can peruse a neuroscience book together or sign up for a web-based course to remain spurred.

7. Break out of your daily practice
Schedules are valuable for keeping up with solid propensities and being useful. In any case, particularly while telecommuting, they can prompt learning latency. It means quite a bit to open yourself to as a wide range of kinds of individuals, circumstances, food sources, scents and sounds as could really be expected. By getting out of your usual range of familiarity, you free yourself up to a wide range of learning potential.One thing I miss, now that we as a whole work from home, is that I don't get presented to close to as various sorts of individuals, circumstances, food sources, scents, and sounds as I used to when I drove.

8. Reflect en route
Reflection concretes learning and provides you with a pride. Great students think back on how far they've come. What kinds of inquiries did you pose? What new knowledge did you get? Where were you absolutely off-base? What amazed you? Evaluating what you know cements

the essentials and gives you a strong groundwork to expand on in the distance. Journaling is an extraordinary method for keeping tabs on your development and monitor fascinating new inquiries you should investigate.

Get support with your learning process
On the off chance that you think the subsequent stage in your process is to begin gaining some new useful knowledge, you're likely correct. Doing so will give many advantages. You'll turn into an all the more balanced individual, become more versatile, and generally speaking have a great time throughout everyday life. So go get that guitar, pursue that stoneware class, or register for that proficient improvement preparing. Begin pursuing a superior you. We will not gloss over it — self-improvement isn't simple all of the time. Yet, discovering some new information doesn't need to be hard. At BetterUp, we can help. In the event that you're put in the effort, we'll assist you with accomplishing your objectives and support you constantly

Advantages of Gaining some new useful knowlege

There are a ton of good, pragmatic motivations to make discovering some new information consistently your propensity, yet the best explanation doesn't have anything to do with common sense — we are learning animals, and the deep rooted practice of realizing makes us people and our lives beneficial. In the event that that hopeful pondering's sufficiently not, here's an additional sensible advantages:

- Advancing across a large number of subjects provides us with a scope of viewpoints to approach in our own tight everyday areas of specialization.
- Learning helps us all the more effectively and promptly adjust to new circumstances.
- A wide information on new circumstances takes care of development by moving us to think imaginatively and giving guides to follow.
- Learning extends our personality and makes us more moving to everyone around us.
- Learning makes us more certain.
- Learning imparts a comprehension of the authentic, social, and regular cycles that effect and cutoff our lives.
- Also, similar to I said, there's the entirety "making like worth living" thing

CHAPTER 10

Set your cash to work

Cash is a device that can assist you with accomplishing your objectives. It can give solace and solidness to your family, make it simpler to anticipate the future, and permit you to save towards significant achievements. In any case, to accomplish these things, you really want to know how to bring in your cash work for you. Making your cash work for you implies assuming command over your funds, then, at that point, utilizing that control to constantly work on your monetary solidness and security. You may ultimately have the option to acquire monetary autonomy or create financial stability through money management. In any case, neither of those things can occur without first comprehension where your cash is proceeding to learn better ways of utilizing it.

Figure out how To Financial plan

A financial plan is a crucial device for fundamentally impacting the manner in which you handle your cash. At the point when you are planning, you comprehend where your cash is coming from and are intentional about where you spend it. You are bringing in your cash do what you believe it should do, as opposed to spending without a plan. When you make a financial plan, you relegate each dollar you procure to a spending classification. You can utilize a spending plan to:
- Decrease your spending
- Comprehend where your cash is going
- Distinguish terrible monetary propensities
- Take care of obligation
- Try not to make new obligation
- Focus on spending on things that are mean quite a bit to you
- Save for the future

Planning is definitely not a one-time activity. It ought to be something you effectively take part in each day. You might have to change your financial plan from one month to another to represent huge costs or your own ways of managing money. At the point when you know the amount of pay you possess, you can choose where to put it. At the point when you are purposeful about where you spend it, you are in charge of your cash. This is the most vital move towards making it work the manner in which you need to, as opposed to feeling constrained by your funds

Escape Obligation

At the point when you are under water, you pay more than the expense of the first buy. You likewise need to create interest installments that can significantly cut into your pay.

Obligation implies your cash isn't working for you, it's going towards paying that premium. It makes a monetary weight and restricts the decisions that you can make.

Taking care of obligation, on the other hand, permits you to take that cash and divert it toward the things that are mean quite a bit to you. You can put it toward other monetary objectives, like putting something aside for training, making a retirement asset, voyaging, or advancing your everyday environment. You can begin a business. You can start money management it, permitting you to develop your abundance and make more monetary solidness and autonomy.

On the off chance that you have a ton of obligation and are feeling overpowered, you can utilize the snowball technique to control the obligation reimbursement process.

- Pay just the base installment on the entirety of your obligations with the exception of the littlest one.
- Put anything additional cash you have toward taking care of the littlest obligation.
- Whenever it's paid off, move onto the following littlest.

As you take care of your more modest obligations, you'll have more cash accessible to take care of your bigger obligations. This force assists you with centering your endeavors and escape obligation more quickly.

Make a Backup stash
Shocks are startling when you don't have control of your funds. A startling vehicle fix, an operation, an employment misfortune, or some other monetary crisis can rapidly send you spiraling into new or more obligation, clearing out any headway you've made towards assuming command over your cash.

Making a secret stash is one more method for bringing in your cash work for you since it implies you have made arrangements for shocks. On the off chance that a crisis comes up, you can give the cash in your asset something to do and recover control of the circumstance.

Building a just-in-case account can take time. Preferably, you ought to save what could be compared to three to a half year of pay. However, every last messed with you can save will help. In the event that you are as yet taking care of obligation or don't have a lot of space for error in your spending plan, put away anything that you can in a "shock costs" class in your financial plan. Toward the month's end, move whatever is in this class to a different investment account.

Note
Put your crisis reserve funds in a high return bank account, which will procure more revenue than a normal saving or financial records. This implies that the cash you set aside will make cash while it's sitting in your financial balance. On the off chance that your bank doesn't offer

high return records or you live in a rustic region without a bank, search for web based financial choices to open a record.

When you are in the clear financially or have more cash free cash in your spending plan, you can set up bigger repeating commitments to develop your rainy day account significantly quicker

Set aside and Put away Your Cash
Whenever you have opened up all the excess cash from taking care of your obligation, you can give your cash something to do through reserve funds and ventures. What you put something aside for will rely upon your age, way of life, and objectives.

Notwithstanding a secret stash, you will likewise require retirement accounts. You ought to likewise consider whether you want:

- Instruction reserve funds, for yourself or your youngsters
- Travel reserve funds
- An initial installment store for a house
- Reserve funds to begin a business
- A vehicle store, for fixes or another vehicle
- Extracurricular asset for wards
- Long haul care investment funds, for yourself or wards

By making assigned investment funds reserves, you can keep tabs on your development toward explicit objectives. You can likewise place those reserve funds in an exorbitant premium record, currency market record or Cd (endorsement of store) to bring in revenue on your cash.

In the event that you won't require your reserve funds for quite a while or many years, one of the most mind-blowing ways of bringing in your cash work for you is to contribute.

At the point when you put your cash into speculations, it develops completely on its own through revenue or the expanded worth of what you put resources into. A few ventures likewise deliver profits, which you can either take as additional pay or reinvest to assist your portfolio with developing .

Robotize your financial plan

In this advanced age, it's presently massively clean to mechanize your cost range in basically every way you can consider, from modernized bill bills, to programmed speculation commitments, with regards to Kenny Senour, authorized money related organizer with Millennial Abundance The executives. "For example, assuming you will likely maximize your Roth IRA in five years, say somewhere in the range of 2022 and 2027 through contributing the generally $6,000, review setting up a computerized commitment of $500 every month," he said. "Mechanizing your spending plan might be a major assist in dealing with your month to month cash with drifting, so any mechanization ought to ideally emerge that very day your check or direct store hits your ledger."

Put resources into Land

On the off chance that you have adequate the means to make down bills on property, making an interest in genuine property is an impeccable way to bring in your cash give you the outcomes you need, expressed Omer Reiner, leader of FL Money Home Purchasers, LLC, a land subsidizing boss.

"At the point when you customize resources," Reiner said, "you deal with the manner in which you need to make cash from it. You can rent it out, fix it up to advance it, transfer worth to development rents, etc."

Put resources into Listed Common Assets

Filed common funds additionally are a marvelous way to develop abundance, exhorted Carter Seuthe, President of Credit Highest point. These cost ranges work through making a venture in basically the same manner in each stock in a given exchange, alongside the Dow Jones or the NASDAQ, he characterized.

"They have continually been demonstrated to beat greatest effectively overseen venture obligations," he expressed, "and accompany the additional advantage of warding off the costs that incorporate broad administration."

Recorded common funds give a generally excellent return without a monstrous amount of risk, he brought.

.Contribute inside the Securities exchange

To earnestly develop your money, your quality bet is to contribute inside the stock market, through shopping individual ETF's (trade exchanged cost range) and shared assets in a "rendition portfolio," as per Johnny Medina, President of Nabla Monetary.

"The standard thought is exceptionally straightforward: Save no less than 10% of your gross profit. Contribute the investment funds with a drawn out term attitude and leave it to intensifying to do the unwinding."

For example, on the off chance that you start with $10,000, get a good deal on a portfolio with the expectation to yield 10%. Following 30 years, you'll have $2.3 million.

Put resources into S&P Assets

One more sort of asset most likely to yield attractive, solid impacts — and which generally yields a middle eleven% yearly return — is the S&P reserve.

As per Andrew Lokenauth, President of Conversant in Money, "The S&P 500 consolidates 500 of America's greatest organizations, across every one of the eleven ventures. Contributing inside the S&P 500 is a smooth and tranquil method for unveiling speculations for the general of people, since you're not making a bet on an unmarried organization, but 500 of America's biggest companies."

Re-Put resources into Yourself to Get More Complex Top level salary Abilities

You might think you really want a PhD to turn into a top level salary proficient, yet at the same that is false all of the time. You can foster more modern abilities and information in your present place of employment by putting resources into yourself. These ventures will give you the information and abilities you really want to get a more modern occupation with more significant compensation. If you have any desire to make a big league salary for your new vocation, then you want to quit mulling over everything as a second job and begin considering it your essential work. You do this by putting time and cash in yourself as long as possible. The profits on these speculations will prompt a lot more lucrative occupation where you can really prosper as an individual as opposed to simply one more pinion in the machine.

Figure out how To Focus on Your Wellbeing and Wellness: Great Wellbeing Is Riches

New goals on the most proficient method to bring in cash work for you are an extraordinary chance to ponder how you can further develop your life in light of the fact that without great wellbeing, improving the advantages of your cash turns into a "mirrage". For the vast majority of us, we don't have the foggiest idea about that being solid is a panacea that can get our independence from the rat race…. Assuming you're similar to the vast majority, this is the kind of thing that you presumably need to develop now and again. Rather than zeroing in more on bringing in cash, why not dedicate some time and assets to improving and supporting steady and better wellbeing status? With regards to working on your wellbeing and wellness, there are a great deal of things that you can do. From being focused on your regular checkup, accepting your meds as recommended, shedding pounds to getting more activity and eating better food sources, there are bunches of easily overlooked details that you can do to hugely affect your life. Regardless of whether you're not at the pinnacle of wellbeing at present, today is the ideal opportunity to set things back up and roll out a few positive improvements. One of the most straightforward however helpful ways of beginning is in the first place a consistent exercise schedule ROUTINE . Assuming you're searching for a few extraordinary tips on how you can develop your actual wellbeing, support your solidarity, energy and improve performance,please investigate this connection

Partake in Your Life And Figure out how To Participate In Vital Sight And Witnessed Occasions

Passing and unanticipated circumstances are invictable, so you want to love the endowment of life and make at any rate a few days noteworthy.

CHAPTER 11

Your wellbeing is your most noteworthy abundance and resource

Your wellbeing is your most noteworthy abundance and resource. Your solid body gives you the strength and energy that assist you with accomplishing improved brings about each part of your life. Having the option to rest around evening time, stroll without torment, eat and appreciate food is the primary significance of joy. Your general wellbeing and prosperity — profound, mental, otherworldly as well as physical — ought to constantly be your main need. Without it, basically nothing else has any significance.

Follow the beneath (Abundance) methodology and make your heath your main concern.

W - Water.

There ought to be no other drink going through your lips other than water. Drinking sufficient water keeps up with the body's liquid equilibrium, which helps transport supplements in the body, direct internal heat level, and summary food.

E - Exercise.

Standard practicing consumes calories and assists you with dealing with your weight. Practice forestalls coronary illness, stroke, diabetes, corpulence, and hypertension. Exercises that include lifting or pushing body weight help to keep up major areas of strength for with

A -Attitude

Begin your day with a solid breakfast. Individuals who have breakfast are less inclined to gorge later in the day. Get a lot of rest. Go for a stroll after supper as opposed to staring at the television. Try not to utilize medications, nicotine, and liquor as a method for adapting to gloomy sentiments and stress.

L - Less pressure.

It is an upsetting world out there! Stress turns into a piece of our cutting edge life and it places our bodies in an uplifted state for an extensive stretch of time, which is truly can quietly hurt our hearts.

Search for ways of decreasing pressure, deal with your time, associate with others and invest energy in living life to the fullest

T - Think positive.

Positive reasoning transforms all issues into open doors; it can further develop the resistant framework works and lessening circulatory strain. Individuals who have positive contemplations pursue better choices and have more trust in themselves.

H - healthy eating

Having an even and solid eating routine can encourage you. Eat more products of the soil. Pick entire grains, similar to oats, entire wheat bread, and earthy colored rice, fish, lean meats, poultry, eggs, sans fat or low-fat milk, cheddar, beans, nuts, and seed. Food high in fat and oil must be totally kept away from. They increment the cholesterol level in the body. Caffeine in the event that consumed in higher sum can cause sleep deprivation and many so its admission must be diminished at any rate. Sound bites can support your energy levels between dinners. Whenever the situation allows, make your tidbits "low-fat" and "low-sugar".

At long last, your body is your precious belonging, deal with it. In this world, being solid is an honor that a few of us appreciate and more often than not we don't perceive how significant it is. Mahatma Gandhi once said that wellbeing is a definitive riches and he was correct. It doesn't make any difference how affluent you are yet in the event that you don't have great wellbeing getting a charge out of life is a struggle. Assuming that there is a way you can contact the existence of an individual and assist them with getting great wellbeing, you will have done significantly more than giving that individual all the wealth in this world.

In agricultural nations, wellbeing is imperative to individuals, yet unfathomably distant In Africa and the vast majority of the emerging nations, wellbeing is crucial to them, yet more often than not it is blocked off. They want to get great and quality medical services, yet the majority of the times their frameworks don't permit it for a large portion of them. Chronic frailty is wild in the African people group, and the greater part of them simply stay there trusting that somebody will come and reduce the unendurable weight from them. It is difficult, and for this reason we as a local area have made it our obligation to guarantee that we help individuals and for the most part youngsters in Africa and the creating scene to get to quality medical services. This is all finished by the altruism of people who understand the circumstances that these individuals in Africa and the emerging nations go through.

Coordinating meetings all through the world pointed toward making wellbeing mindfulness can go far in aiding these individuals. For instance there are numerous global meetings on general wellbeing all over the planet. These meetings assist individuals with understanding what the creating scene is going through in regards to admittance to great and quality medical services frameworks. A genuine test must be tended to by everybody on the planet until everybody knows and they begin taking care of business. Data shared at these gatherings are vital and add to great wellbeing, however, without a doubt, not very many, if by any means, individuals from Africa or emerging nations can join in and access the relevant data spread in that. On the off chance that you don't have great wellbeing, this is a constraint like no other throughout everyday life. The weight of chronic weakness and sicknesses block a many individuals from prevailing throughout everyday life. Bunches of human resources and possibilities is restricted by weight of infections

Individuals in Africa and the creating scene have a great deal of possibilities that is restricted by these sicknesses and lightening the weight for them makes a big difference to them and the local area they will develop to serve. Whenever an illness removes a youngster from the local area, they lose the kid, yet they likewise lose the open door they needed to appreciate what these children would have developed to turn into. Assist with saving lives today and hold hands with us as we attempt and get these individuals the opportunity to appreciate life to the greatest. Wellbeing is Abundance' Maxim implies that the condition of prosperity, liberated from illness or sicknesses, both physical and mental is without a doubt a riches. The Proverb is an old one, as can be seen from an incredible Old style Rome Writer, Virgil's (Publius Vergilius Maro) Saying - 'The Best Abundance is Wellbeing'. Virgil is considered to have experienced terrible wellbeing all through his life and maybe it is conceivable that the situation with his wellbeing roused him to present this saying as a useful tidbit for the approaching ages. Essentially, a Spanish Maxim goes this way - 'A man who is excessively occupied to deal with his wellbeing resembles a technician excessively occupied to deal with his instruments'. For most of us 'Abundance' signifies having bunches of cash, a major land parcel, gems, vehicles, a homestead, a level, a house or any property which has a capability of having money related esteem on the lookout. However, this restricts the degree and vision of the term 'Riches', however, in the regular sense and word reference definition, it is especially adept. Yet, assuming we expand our reasoning and look past our restricted vision towards 'Riches', we will see and observe that, abundance isn't simply just the thing is being said about it. To more readily comprehend this, how about we notice our own lives. We learn at school, school or have a calling and the 'Information' and 'Experience' acquired in this climate is additionally a 'Riches', however you can't contact or feel 'Information' and 'Experience', like money. Here, it is an abundance as in it has a worth which is reasonable, regarded and respected in different social conditions. Additionally, you can likewise make more abundance with the utilization of 'Unusual Riches'. Among different types of such Whimsical Abundance comes 'Wellbeing' which is by a long shot the main abundance one can have, pretty much at the very level as that of 'Profound Wellbeing'. This brings into light, the way that 'Abundance' is really reliant and connected with 'Wellbeing' in more than one manner, that's what a straightforward model is - assuming you are genuinely and deranged, you can not work as expected or not work by any stretch of the imagination. Furthermore, on the off chance that you can't work in the ideal way you can not obtain the ideal measure of abundance. It can't be expressed on the other hand about wellbeing being subject to riches, essentially in light of the fact that to be solid, there is not really any capital included except if you pay to be prepared for staying fit. Having declared that it isn't astute to be 'Unwealthy' to be 'Solid', for example try not to get fixated on wellbeing so much that it turns into an obstacle towards your useful limit with respect to riches. Wellbeing is as much a riches and a significant one, whose worth is conceivable by the individuals who really think of it as a riches and in addition to a prevailing fashion. The people who have not understood this need to think harder.

For what reason did the Wellbeing call Abundance?
Wellbeing is an abundance in view of its diverse advantages which affect our lives, some of which might have been not understood at this point. The advantages which have been understood, point straightforwardly towards the reality of this reality and lay out it as a Reality.

- Wellbeing is the Establishment for other Riches - Wellbeing and abundance are connected in numerous ways. Yet, one truth that stands apart among all, is that wellbeing itself advances abundance. A solid individual will be more dynamic, savvy and proficient, this straightforwardly influences his capacity to bring in more and this cash can be additionally used in making more riches.

- **Wellbeing is a Speculation with Great Returns:** Wellbeing is one venture which has deep rooted enduring returns. This is clear from the way that - Individuals impacted with terrible wellbeing frequently bite the dust early in life. They have been investing all their energy in securing riches and overlooking wellbeing. Their 'Profession Life' was great however it ended up being as harvesting since they are not any more alive. Added to the way that many don't sufficiently live to gather the annuity and different advantages for which they spent a lifetime working. The facts confirm that passing is unavoidable and eccentric however the chances of biting the dust right on time as the hands of an illness increment more without any a solid way of life. On the other hand talking a sound individual is bound to live longer and receive the rewards of his persistent effort over the long haul as well as the short run. A sound way of life will get him far from most sicknesses and they could try and give their abundance to survivors and main beneficiaries and even advantage them.

- **Solid Populace Contributes towards Sound Economy:** Sound Populace straightforwardly contributes towards an advanced economy of the separate country. It is extremely straightforward this - on the off chance that the workers of an association are unfortunate or infected, the benefits of the association will descend or remain business as usual. This won't just influence the association it will additionally influence the income produced through these. A country's economy can help just while its supporting construction is in great shape. The better the part of the construction the better will be the result. A model towards this viewpoint was featured by a new report directed by the World Wellbeing Association. As per the review, around 47% of the labor force in urbanized modern circumstances is overweight. Around 27% of those reviewed experience the ill effects of hypertension and around 10% are diabetic. The review found that laborers are at amore serious gamble of creating persistent illnesses, for example, weight, coronary failure, stroke, and malignant growth. One needn't bother with a well-qualified's viewpoint to envision the future of such a modern set-up.

- **Wellbeing is a way to Better Living:** Great wellbeing naturally empowers to expand our body's ability and the subsequent inclination to secure chances to procure more and live better. makes one a superior individual genuinely as well as intellectually too.

Monetary security and wellbeing are emphatically connected with individual bliss and to each other. A solid mindset advances great qualities like difficult work, sharing, graciousness, discipline and other positive characteristics. Then again, unfortunate life is a wellspring of troubled life. A well off individual might have every one of the extravagances of life yet it doesn't be guaranteed to imply that he is carrying on with a decent life. Better living is just gained by understanding that 'Wellbeing is a method of Better Living', foundation wise as well as by mentality wise.

- **Sound Psyche Stays in a Solid Body:** It is valid definitely - knowledge, imagination, the common sense, humor, modesty, show, correspondence and different parts of the brain are not simply practice subordinate, they are likewise reliant upon solid way of life. A functioning body empowered by the actual system, adjusted diet, reflection and asking makes inspirational tones, invigorates and stimulates our mind. It improves the exhibition of the mind in all issues of life, with which one can accomplish more prominent levels and rouse others to do likewise.

- **Counteraction is Superior to Fix**: There is a platitude that 'Exercise is the Best Medication', it has not been said very much like that. The saying stands firm on its ground; legitimate activity is a major obstruction to illness, everything being equal. Practice physical, mental and profound all further develop resistance and make us more grounded. We will be less inclined to experience the ill effects of diseases, sensitivities, stress and different issues influencing our wellbeing. All the more critically, it demonstrates the familiar adage that 'Anticipation is Superior to Fix'. The cash and energy spent on visiting and purchasing medication might have been forestalled assuming we had adhered to the fundamental rule. The greater part of us don't want to take a gander at our wellbeing, it is just when we get impacted that we will generally focus on the bigger issue. The fix likewise includes some significant downfalls and can influence an individual's wellbeing considerably further. For instance, the high use as well as late hospital expenses can cause actual side effects of pressure, for example headaches, a sleeping disorder, and uneasiness. On the off chance that the individual is all prepared shy of assets he is probably going to experience monetary trouble too. Indeed, even extensive result like unfortunate record as a consumer or potentially insolvency and decreased pay can muddle what is going on significantly more. Preventive estimates like appropriate activity, great rest, suggested diet, normal check-ups and so forth are superior with the outcomes of not complying to this straightforward rule of life.

- **Cash Set aside is Cash Procured:** Having a decent wellbeing is a 'Valuable Cash Saving Plan' basically on the grounds that the cash which would have been used in the treatment of sicknesses and it's unified costs has been presently saved or potentially used in additional reserve funds. There are a few cases where the treatment of a sickness makes individuals bankrupt and make the destitute. If by some stroke of good luck they had tuned in and followed the savvy words, their use would have been saved.

- **Counteraction of Hostile to Social Exercises and Persistent vices:** Liquor addiction, smoking, illicit drug use, and other criminal propensities will generally be moderated or non-existent among the specialists of a solid way of life. Eagerness, envy, scorn, retribution and other gloomy feelings will generally be disturbed when one is 'Cash Disapproved'. For such people, everything revolves around getting what they need, either no holds barred. Their psyches are ruined and focussed on obtaining a lot of riches, this inclination cultivates further bothersome practices which influence even the incorrupt brain. Certain people begin to take liquor, tranquilizes and enjoy unbridled conduct to unwind. Nonetheless, the outcomes of such demonstrations are consistently horrendous even to the individuals who are not straightforwardly connected with that individual. A sound individual knows the outcomes due to his canny psyche and as such won't just swear off these yet will likewise attempt to forestall these to benefit the general public. With respect to the ones who have endure such exercises, are now capable and reluctant to do likewise.

- **Makes Life really Satisfying:** Wellbeing is one thing which incorporates every one of the constructive outcomes that can make one's life a satisfying one. The individuals who have perceived to work out some kind of harmony among wellbeing and abundance have a sound psyche. It is reflected in their way of behaving and demeanor. They are bound to carry on with life in a preferable manner over the people who aren't sound. We can partake in all parts of life just when we have the opportunity and energy to do as such. A condition of prosperity establishes such a climate where one can zero in on all parts of his existence without being grieved or fretted over it. For a solid individual, even a little green leaf can bring happiness.

- **Wellbeing makes a Superior Society:** Solid individuals create a superior society. Adjusted people comply with the principles, advance harmony, coordinate, be capable, accomplish charitable effort, enjoy useful exercises and other significant exercises which make a general public a superior spot to live. This lays out as well as reestablishes respectability in the public arena. It is just when the individual is satisfied with his life that he will contemplate others in the public arena. The way of behaving and exercises of such individuals advance comparable feelings straightforwardly and by implication along all times of individuals.

For what reason don't we heed the Astute Guidance?

Like all great guidelines of life that are intended to be observed, wellbeing is something which we take nonchalantly and on occasion don't make a big deal about it. As far as some might be concerned, it's past the point where it is possible to act and as far as some might be concerned, there is still time. Whatever, the circumstance or disposition, human propensity to succumb to simplicity and solace leads to negative inclinations.

- **Profession Driven Life:** With regards to vocation versus wellbeing, we picked a vocation, attentively or coincidentally. All through our lives, profession has been featured as the something significant which we need to accomplish in our life. Nonetheless, we neglect to put a light on the enormous capability of wellbeing in our day to day existence as well as in our profession. In some cases, the message of the vocation becomes stronger than wellbeing and it is overlooked out and out. In this way starts a lifelong life - where they need to sit for extended periods of time, work like insects and furthermore get taken advantage of all the while. Unfit to adjust our requirement for work out, sustenance, entertainment and other everyday errands, we begin carrying on with a day to day existence which is entirely or exclusively rotating around our endlessly work alone. Large numbers of us go much further, we labor for 24 hours per day, every one of the 7 days without break, to acquire our meat and potatoes. Really buckling down isn't terrible yet at the expense of our wellbeing and lives is absolutely improper. On the off chance that we continue to work without making a harmony between our work and wellbeing, when will we get an opportunity to relish achievement? This kind of life produces large, hypertensive and powerless people.

- **Absence of Time**: This is the most widely recognized excuse for not having the option to give time to wellbeing. For the overwhelming majority of us, this is valid, we are so profoundly soaked in our work that we even rush and proportion our day to day errands like washing garments, eating a legitimate dinner or skipping breakfast. Additionally, we, resort to inexpensive food and other debasing exercises like awkward late night parties, social affairs, etc. Our timetable is full and wellbeing isn't even on the rundown. We are so caught up in these that we lack opportunity and energy to contemplate and additionally plan it in our lives. So we drop the thought, all together. There is dependably time, all we want is the executives and responsibility.

- **Illness Free means Sound**: There is an enormous segment of the public which has an off-base idea that in the event that they are not experiencing any sickness, they are solid and don't have to stress over it. Simply being without sickness is something to be thankful for yet to keep up with the infection free body will sometime require endeavors. Everything around us has a day to day existence; this condition of illness through and through freedom likewise not keep going long until and except if we make the fitting strides. Not to forget on the grounds that you feel that you have no sickness may not be guaranteed to imply that you don't have one. Go for normal check-ups to try not to be under a plausible wrong impression.

- **Youth Mindset**: I'm youthful, I needn't bother with any activity, is the typical youth attitude. Also, they find practice and related exercises exhausting, everyday and tedious movement. Youngsters and the same for the most part have a decent wellbeing since they carry on with a planned life where actual work is likewise involved. Nonetheless, it isn't actually the case that being youthful implies that you don't require work out. Normal activity both mental and actual makes one a superior and more grounded individual. A system created as of now turns into a standard propensity which one might proceed with for his entire life.

- **Sluggishness**: Urbanization fuelled by innovation has made us languid. We drive in vehicles since it is advantageous and efficient, we eat cheap food, since we would rather not cook, we have workers who take care of our day to day tasks and we sit before our PC's or TV; playing or watching unscripted TV dramas. Throughout some undefined time frame, this large number of elements have made us lethargic and proclaimed inactive way of life. In this universe of instant, we could do without to try sincerely as it seems, by all accounts, to be obsolete particularly when we have the innovation to carry out play out our responsibilities.Easy routes: another time of wellbeing items has been flooding the market, professing to make you solid while sitting in your homes. We have natural teas, stomach exhausts, sauna belts, figure enhancers, body conditioning machines and so forth. Every one of these not just advance sluggishness, they likewise project that great wellbeing can be accomplished through easy routes. In any case, there is no easy route to difficult work, difficult work itself is the main alternate way. These items are problematic and they are valuable in nature. They are no options in contrast to ordinary strategies for working out.

- **Captives to our Propensities**: Persistent vices Fanatic, the statement is valid. Vices are difficult to break since they have turned into a piece of our mind and body for a significant stretch of time. From one perspective, we, have dangerous propensities like smoking, drinking and so forth, there are different propensities like dozing late, observing late night on everyday schedule, stuck to interpersonal organization and so on, which aren't perilous yet can disturb a sound way of life.

- **Protection from Change**: Bringing an end to our persistent vices takes time, it can't be accomplished in one go. It is a continuous interaction and one which could require more exertion than what is possible. Our bodies are versatile and they likewise adjust rapidly towards our unfortunate behavior patterns. Our day to day propensities become our daily practice and ever-present reiteration makes them considerably more grounded. At the point when we attempt to change this framework, our bodies are not adjusted to a sound way of life and subsequently, there is solid obstruction. This opposition fluctuates from one person to another and in view of the degree of enslavement.

- **Reliance on Meds**: In this speedy world, we lack opportunity and energy to practice however we really have the opportunity to visit a specialist and get help from our ills. The greater part of the prescriptions are pain relievers, they kill the aggravation yet don't eliminate the illness and it's re-event. But since we really want prompt help we find it advantageous to pop a pill instead of stroll for thirty minutes. Then, at that point, there are the people who are occupied to such an extent that they couldn't visit a specialist to treat themselves; they remove the-counter medication. Drugs give prompt alleviation from our aggravation and sufferings yet would it say it are the correct method for managing your medical issues? In no way, shape or form, persistent issues truly do require an expert assistance yet those having normal issues can dispose of their concerns with the straightforward timetable of routine work-out.

- **Negative Wellspring of Motivation:** Almost certainly, that wellbeing is helpful however the criticisers sound way of life is continuously tracking down the reason to fight for their own flawed way of life. Instances of the individuals who keep on experiencing illnesses even subsequent to following a daily schedule of activity. Yet, who can say for sure what level of infection is one experiencing, how long will it require to come to a typical level and is the activity is being done appropriately. Then, there are individuals who actually have pot tummies regardless of strolling or running for a long time. Here it is to be perceived that we don't have full information and we rush to make judgment calls.

How to make Wellbeing a Riches?
Making wellbeing an abundance isn't inconceivable, however it tends to be more diligently. However at that point, there is no mischief in doing a thing which should be possible without any problem.

- **Trust in the Maxim:** To deal with it, you want to trust in it. Accepting and reaffirming this idea is the most effective way to make 'Wellbeing is Abundance' your Mantra. Confidence in something makes that thing achievable and furthermore rouses your endeavors. Tune in or watch wellbeing based projects or writing to summon and motivate a craving to accomplish your point. Think about great wellbeing as a pathway to progress in varying backgrounds. Conviction is additionally fortified by move made on the drive.

- **Follow up on the Guidance:** When we feline on the exhortation we are laying out an establishment for good wellbeing. You don't have to do anything unique. Well conceived plan out your system and follow it. You need to comprehend that it is a day to day undertaking in the event that not 5-6 days of an issue in seven days. One of the least expensive ways of seeking after a decent wellbeing is to get up promptly in the first part of the day and just walk, run or run. The main venture one requires is a decent sets of shoes. Concerning mental activity, one can contemplate by sitting and shutting eyes and consider nothing for 15-30 minutes for a beginning. Moreover one can likewise perform petitions. Likewise take a decent eating regimen, which incorporates organic products, vegetables and other nutritious feed consistently. One can likewise practice at home by utilizing treadmills, cycling, individual rec center and through different exercises.
- **Strong Responsibility**: To keep a sound way of life, one requirements a solid responsibility, not really for a week or a month, but rather for a lifetime. At first, we are completely siphoned up for a week or only for a day. From that point onward, we are back to our stationary way of life. Dealing with one's wellbeing ought to be a ceaseless interaction and not broken into parts. We really want to follow a daily schedule of activities and legitimate food. To commit a solid responsibility, never surrender, consistently attempt over and over; regardless of how frequently you could fall flat. Make a normal exerciser your inspiration, notice and follow the example, if vital put your own thoughts into it. Moreover one can join a companion or a colleague in a wellness system, this way you will get the excitement to stay committed in light of the fact that now you are

a group and answerable for one another. Make your inadequacies, apprehension about sickness or anything which can be utilized to go about as a wellspring of responsibility

- **Try not to propel yourself excessively Hard:** Frequently we have every one of the devices to stay solid yet we need or don't matter the methods in a legitimate way. Try not to go over the top with it or hurriedly as it can bring about unwanted outcomes. Relax, you are not in a rivalry. In an energized mode, we frequently exaggerate specific exercises which tire us or sickness us. The best thing do is start with straightforward things and increment the force and term up to a reasonable stage. Try not to attempt an excessive number of things on the double, center around a specific sort of activity as opposed to enjoying all. Keep in mind 'Unwavering mindsets always win in the end'.

- **Change your Way of life:** Tweaking your way of life extraordinarily influences your wellbeing in a positive way. Once in a while we simply have to change our standard undertakings to be solid, such as dozing early and getting up right on time. This standard itself makes adequate opportunity to make an equilibrium in our exercises. Then, at that point, we can change our eating routine example and amount to suit individual requirements. It isn't important to eat anything the entire family eats. Eat what suits you the best in light of conference with a nutritionist or specialist. Progressively get a healthy equilibrium the time given to your profession, actual wellness, relationship with others, monetary position, profound viewpoint, climate and any remaining perspectives. Enjoy your lethargic way of life just, when seven days with the goal that your ongoing routine doesn't become exhausting.

- **Look for Proficient Assistance:** A few people require a specific push or certain circumstances under which he compels himself to seek after a solid way of life. This work can be highlighted by Nutritionist, Fitness coach, Wellness Master, Rehabilitative Experts, Wellness Mentor, Exercise room, etc. Large numbers of us have no clue about how to begin or what to do, it is here that expert assistance proves to be useful and proper. Burning through cash on wellbeing itself persuades us to be a customary in our expertly directed everyday practice. This is on the grounds that we know and cognizant about the way that we have put away some cash; it shouldn't go waste.

- **Access Wellbeing Assets:** The wellbeing based material is accessible in different structures - books, DVDs, electronic contraptions, machines, magazines, papers, TV, radio, web et al. While a portion of these are efficiently and effectively accessible on the web, libraries, and TV, others are costly. For the people who can't head outside or feel complex can practice through High impact exercise Video accessible in video stores, web, and TV. These have work out regimes which can be followed basically by impersonating the activities. Peruse and follow the wellbeing articles and utilize specific contraptions to enhance your pervasive wellbeing program.

- **Bring Varieties**: After a specific timeframe, certain activities will quite often lose or become incapable in keeping us as sound as we need or as we ought to. In this way look for elective wellsprings of activity or vitiate your program. In the event that are exhausted you can seek after different exercises which welcome a new methodology and impact on wellbeing. Explore and be innovative, blend 2 or 3 kind of wellbeing exercises according to your comfort. You can make your regular routine tasks your activity too, tidying up a room can be acted in a cadenced way to make it fascinating or accomplish something which you haven't done for some time, such as playing a round of cricket or chess. You can likewise bring variety into your day to day daily schedule, as once in each while taking a cycle to the workplace rather than a vehicle. These little endeavors deliver huge profits.

- **Be your own Tutor**: Frequently we join a work out regime with our companions and frequently it happens that main successor interest begins to wind down after a specific timeframe. Peer impact here can divert us from our objective, we may fell solitary or we could get baffled when our assigned accomplice doesn't uphold us or loses interest. Here, we ought to continuously remember that come what may, you will follow your daily practice. Try not to depend a lot on others, expect that your affiliation may not keep going long, appreciate it while it endures and be free.

www.ingramcontent.com/pod-product-compliance
Lightning Source LLC
Chambersburg PA
CBHW080951220526
45465CB00008BA/3243